James May is a writer, broadcaster and co-host of BBC's *Top Gear*. He writes a weekly column for the *Daily Telegraph* and has presented series for the BBC, ITV, Channel 4 and Sky.

JAMES MAY
CAR FEVER

The car bore's essential companion

HODDER

The contents of this book first appeared in James May's
Daily Telegraph and *Top Gear Magazine* columns.

First published in Great Britain in 2009 by Hodder & Stoughton
An Hachette UK company

First published in paperback in 2010

2

ISBN 978 0 340 99455 9

Typeset in Excelsior by Palimpsest Book Production Limited,
Grangemouth, Stirlingshire

Printed and bound in the UK by Clays Ltd, St Ives plc

Hodder & Stoughton policy is to use papers that are natural,
renewable and recyclable products and made from wood grown in sustainable
forests. The logging and manufacturing processes are expected to
conform to the environmental regulations of the country of origin.

Hodder & Stoughton Ltd
338 Euston Road
London NW1 3BH

www.hodder.co.uk

To SFfD

Contents

Introduction

I feel that a book full of secondhand newspaper columns about motoring should begin with an apology, so here goes.

I'd like to apologise for that shirt I'm wearing on the cover. I know, from reading comments on the electric interweb, that many people feel quite strongly about that shirt, log its appearances on TV, discuss its sartorial merits, and implore me to get rid of it. But it isn't that simple.

You will see, if you read 'Old bag dies after 25 years as my friend' on page 165, that I had hitherto regarded my deceased Adidas rucksack as my constant fabric companion on this uncharted journey we call life. I now realise that it was the shirt.

That shirt is now me. It is the means by which my friends recognise me, and next to which my face performs only a secondary reserve role. It would be missed if it wasn't there.

Other shirts come and go quite quickly, because they shrink, tear, get left in hotels, sustain a curry injury, and so on. But this shirt refuses to give up its shirty duties. It has at least two holes in it, it's pretty threadbare, and the cuffs are badly frayed, but it just carries on. One day I will cough and it will turn into a puff of vapour to be carried away on the breeze, but until then I might as well wear it.

I could never discard a perfectly good shirt, or even a perfectly awful one if it still fits and covers up my unsightly nipples. My cleaner has taken the executive decision to turn other old shirts of mine into dusters and car polishing rags, but I have expressly forbidden her ever to do such a thing to this one.

It is the first shirt I ever bought specifically for TV appearances, and has now lasted so long, and been to so many places around the world, that it has become talismanic, like a raven at a historic building. I now take this shirt on every trip, even if I don't actually intend to wear it. For *Top Gear's* North Pole trip I obviously had to pack a lot of noisy and unflattering cold weather protective clothing, but The Shirt was in my rucksack all the same, to protect me.

A shirt, I suspect, is a little like a cat that is allowed to go outside. There's always the risk that it will be run over, but if it survives the first six months, then it's wise enough to survive into old age. Some shirts live only for a few glorious weeks before they are cruelly snatched away by the unforgiving and indiscriminate hand of shirt fate. This shirt has already lasted for six years of almost uninterrupted use, so I reckon it will be with me until the end.

At a rough guess, because even I'm not boring enough to keep a record of this sort of thing, this shirt has been washed and ironed over 500 times and has travelled at least 125,000 miles, or about half way to the moon. Yet by my calculations it is only one third of the way through its projected life, which means it should last for another 12 years. But I can easily eke that out to 15.

What really amazes me though, is that until I saw the cover design for this book, I hadn't really considered the significance of the blue flowery shirt in the formation of my character. I now realise that I don't really have any sort of job at all. Only my shirt does. I am not my body. I am not even my mind. I am merely the vessel that my shirt is wrapped around, and, as Oscar Wilde might have said, if this shirt goes, then so do I.

I hope you enjoy the motoring adventures of the blue flowery shirt as much as my shirt enjoyed writing it.

May's Britain, a broad sunlit upland

When I'm in power, there are going to be some changes around here, I can tell you. May's Britain is going to be a better place to live.

It's all a matter of passing some very simple and patently quite overdue laws. For a start, there will be strict penalties for any eating establishment that serves normal food in a bowl, and indeed for anyone who writes 'eating establishment' instead of 'restaurant'.

Now: food in a bowl is quite acceptable if it's one of those one-utensil, one-implement meals. Some pastas, for example; chilli con carne, cornflakes, stew, Spam and beans. But anyone caught presenting a pork chop and vegetables in something clearly intended for soup will go to prison for one year.

Similarly, the proprietor of any local who arranges sausage and mash in an artful way, instead of forming the mash into a neat Mount Fuji and inserting the sausages into it in the style of the *Dandy*, will be made to eat pizza and work in a municipal scullery until he or she renounces gastropubbery. No one can deny that this will make the country a better place.

And it's not just about food; there's more, from the field of retail. This week, with a mate, I have tried camping for the first time in many years, and, having disposed of my childhood tent long ago in a part-exchange deal against some bicycle spares, decided to buy a new one.

The man in the camping shop described the one I eventually

chose (from a picture in a book) as a two-stroke-three-man tent. I believed him. He may have believed it himself. But once it was erected it became quite clear that it was barely big enough for one normal bloke, or at a pinch two who like each other a lot. It tapered towards one end, causing unwanted intimacy, and was very low. Furthermore, the sleeping bag he sold me was also tapered, and quite patently based on a sleep-deprivation torture designed by Chairman Mao to make political prisoners confess.

Apparently, these features enhance the chances of survival in sub-zero temperatures and howling winds on the north face of a mountain. Yet the purveyor of tents must have known, when he saw me, that I was the sort of man who never imagined that a tent could be anything other than triangular in section, and who would assume a sleeping bag to be rectangular.

Fine. In May's Britain he will be allowed to continue selling such tents. But only after he has lived in one for six months.

See? Some simple rules based on jeopardy will cure our society of many of its creeping blights while ridding it of the hideous spectre of liability-based legislation. I'm not going to concern myself with the funding of the health service, immigration or the housing crisis. I'll use the appropriate experts for these. I will just concentrate on those small, nagging irritations that ruin our lives out of all proportion.

Here's another one. A man outside my window has just started using one of those petrol-engine leaf-blowers. This is a truly fatuous piece of kit. The leaves are all over his garden because nature blew them there in the first place, and blowing them around some more will achieve nothing other than the complete ruination of my day. He's just making a horrible noise and annoying everyone within a two-mile radius, which means he's caused more distress in the community than a burglar who merely robs one house. Prison. One year.

Obviously, I have some plans to make life better and fairer for the motorist, too. I'm not going to clamp down on speed cameras or road tolls, I'm not going to ban caravans, there will be no punishment for driving in the middle lane of an empty motorway, and I'm not going to do anything at all about untaxed vehicles. These things are not bothering me much.

But traffic wardens seem to be more aggressive, more pedantic, and more superior than ever. The 'parking enforcement officer' has become almost untouchable in Britain, and has been elevated to some spurious moral high ground that brooks no contest and admits no latitude. So I have a plan.

If you apply for a job as a traffic warden, you will immediately be sent to one of my new prisons. There you will sew mail bags, slop out for your colleagues, and take part in a weekly day-release programme of community service activities to help the old, the infirm, and the disadvantaged.

And when you have proved yourself to be honest, socially upstanding and of spotless character, you will be released, given a hat, and permitted to stand in judgement on others' fallibility.

But not before.

Italian engine, charismatic, would like to meet small Japanese sports car for shed frolics

A car I still admire, even after the twelve years that have passed since I had one as a company car in a proper job that I went to every day, is the Alfa Romeo 164 3.0 V6.

Even if you noticed them at the time, you may have forgotten that the 164 ever existed. There certainly aren't many of them around any more, and whenever I've tried to find a good one during an attack of car fever, I've only ever been able to locate a complete snotter. So I forgot about the 164 as well.

But then, a few weeks ago, we devised another of our *Top Gear* challenges; one of those that requires us each to buy a car for £1000. I suggested – silly, really – that I'd quite like an Alfa Romeo 164 3.0. So the researchers, who are pretty good at this sort of thing, went to work on the World Wide Web of Lies and came up with a tidy-looking top-spec Cloverleaf model even before I'd got back from the newsagents with *Autotrader*.

So we bought it, I took it for a drive, and it's still pretty good. The undercarriage of this 170,000-miler was perhaps a bit sloppy, and I'm sure the gearchange was crisper on the one I had, but it was still quite magical. What's more, and contrary to the reputation old Alfas have, everything on it still worked: the air-con, the curious keyboard controls for the fan and heater, the interior lights, the seat motors – the lot. The interior was excellent.

Next, we put it up on ramps and had a good look around

underneath. Very solid. No leaks. No signs of crash damage. I found a small patch of rot, about the size of my thumb, where a door seal had perished and created a water trap, but it represented no more than two hundred pounds worth of repair work. Here, at last, was a good Alfa 164.

And so, in accordance with the rules of the challenge, I sawed it in two. From a technical point of view this was quite difficult, and I was obliged to wear some safety glasses in case I was hit in the eye by half a car. It was even more difficult emotionally, as I wanted to keep it the way its maker had intended and even in my garage.

Exactly why I had to saw it in half I can't tell you, because it's secret and I don't want to spoil the forthcoming moment of 'TV comedy gold' when it rolls on to your screens*. You can be reasonably certain, though, that the whole episode will not end elegantly and that the two halves of the 164 will never be satisfactorily reunited. I'm fairly heartbroken.

On the other hand, I do know the rules of this competition and I'm fairly confident that the best bit of the 164, the engine, will survive. And this had me thinking. A week later I drove an original Mazda MX-5 around a small racing circuit, and was reminded of what a great car it is. Then I wondered how much better it would be with the Alfa engine installed.

Would it fit? The wit of man when it comes to forcing things into places where they weren't designed to go – anchovies inside olives, for example – knows no bounds. From a practical and geometric point of view, my piano should never have made it up my dog-legged staircase and into my sitting room. But it did and so, under the terms of the deal I struck with the piano shop, I had to buy it.

I really like the idea. The balance and rear-drive response of the little Japanese roadster, the vivacity and muscle of Italy's most charismatic V6. I'm sure there would be a few

---

*It became one half of my Alfa-Saab push-me-pull-you limo.

dimensional and weight issues, but it's no more ridiculous than shoe-horning a big V8 into the AC Ace to make the Cobra, or yet another big V8 into the Sunbeam Alpine to make the Tiger. It must be possible.

Of course, Mazda or Alfa Romeo would never consider such a thing. They're rivals, they have no tie-ups, and the process would be fraught with the sort of legal and logistical obstacles that only massive corporations can put in their own paths.

But Britain is festooned with the sort of business that thrives on this sort of thing. I'm not talking about Lotus or Prodrive, or even Williams engineering. I mean men in sheds.

Men in sheds were the cornerstone of this nation's industrial greatness, and men in sheds are its most enduring legacy. They're still there, mending, making, inventing and confronting accepted practice. Some of them are even making cars, and one of them could build me a Mazda Romeo.

Morgan, I mean you.

Old things – not as good as they once were

A common feature in a Sunday newspaper supplement is the one in which some person of significance describes his or her typical day. You know the sort of thing: get up at such and such a time, unlock the kids' bedroom, eat this, do that, meet these people, and so on.

These articles drive me up the wall. For one thing, no one important ever seems to do anything, which makes me wonder how they came to be so influential that a newspaper wants to talk to them. Secondly, they're always thinly disguised boasts about how Fairtrade the coffee is, or how sophisticated the home appliances. There's always far too much mention of the juicer for my liking.

So, by way of contrast, I bring you a life in the Sunday of a slightly sad middle-aged bloke with a debilitating enthusiasm for mechanical items powered by internal combustion engines. It's not good and is intended as a warning.

The plan was simple. Make my way to the local flying club, using one of the nine modes of personal transport available to me, and go for a flip in the tenth, my little light aircraft. So we begin in the garage with my modest collection of classic motorcycles.

Most recent addition to this lot is my 1968 Honda CB250 twin. I like old Hondas a lot, and had been looking for one of these for a bit. Eventually I found one that a bloke had restored beautifully but couldn't make run properly, and so, exploiting his despair, I knocked him down substantially on the asking price on the basis that I'd be able to sort it back home.

And I did, after about three months, eventually tracing the fault to a tiny missing rubber bung inside one of the carburettors. The 250 burst into life, after a spot of fooling about with jump leads and a booster pack. It was even running on both cylinders! So off I went.

But within a mile I was rewarded with a damp leg, the result of petrol spouting from the carb assembly like some ornamental fuel fountain. But not to worry, because I have two more old Hondas. My early-60s C200, for example; a simple machine of 90cc and an uplifting, prosaic experience. The least a motorcycle can be while still technically being one. This turned out to be as dead as Jacob Marley in *A Christmas Carol*, that is, as a doornail.

So I turned to the 1972 CB500 Four, one of the finest products ever to come from Soichiro Honda's bid for two-wheeled world domination. After reassembling it and extracting it from the back of the garage, I pressed the starter button and something exploded in the bowels of its complex four-pot motor. But at least moving that out of the way had given me access to the Moto Guzzi V11, which I've owned from new for many years and maintained fastidiously.

Obviously that didn't work, because it was built near Lake Como in northern Italy, a place famous for ice-cream and ancient chapels dedicated to St Anthony, the patron saint of things that are lost. So finally, after several hours of trying, I was forced onto the seat of my Triumph Speed Triple which, being new, started immediately.

But then Woman turned up and demanded to be taken to the airfield as well, and as she hates motorcycles this meant turning my attention to the cars. The old Bentley is a nice way to travel on a sunny day of fun, but technically it's for sale as I've bought an old Rolls-Royce instead. And the fuel gauge is broken. Meanwhile, the Royce isn't here yet because it's away with a man who's re-lacquering the cracked dashboard, after which it's in for some engine work.

The Porsche, then. It's my poshest car and a convertible to boot, and just the sort of thing in which a chap and his gal might arrive at an airfield. No, not the Porsche, because one of the windows has stuck in the open position so it can't be parked anywhere. And so, some three hours after I stepped out of my front door, we set off in the Fiat Panda.

And it didn't end there. At the airfield, I uncovered my Luscombe 8 monoplane, an American-built machine of 1946 vintage. In its time, it was a radical aeroplane, the first all-metal light aircraft, something that could live outdoors without fear of the wings rotting away or anything like that. It is in excellent condition and has been rigorously serviced for its entire life, as you would demand of an aircraft.

I spent the usual half a lifetime on my pre-flight checks, fuelled up, strapped in and ran through the start-up procedure. The 100hp air-cooled flat-four roared into lustful life. I taxied to the end of the runway, did some more checks for full power, oil pressure and all the rest of it and then opened the throttle.

Halfway down the runway I was rewarded with what I regard as a porthole to the sublime; a view of a perfect English heaven, seen through the screen of a classic aeroplane in the moment it lifts from the grass at the historic White Waltham airfield. And then, at 800 feet, the engine cut out. Not permanently – it just faltered for a few seconds and then picked up again – but even so I nearly soiled myself. Five minutes later I was back on the deck covering it up again.

The message here is quite simple. All this old stuff is rubbish. None of it works properly. After almost a whole day of fart-arsing around with machinery I was forced to conclude that the only dependable things in my life are an Italian car and a British motorcycle. No one would have bet on that.

And here's the advice. Buy one new car, any car, and use that for everything. Then you can devote the rest of your life to something useful.

How not to drive like an Italian

As I've always understood things, there is only one way to drive a small Fiat; and that is without mercy.

Here's how to do it. Select first, lift the clutch abruptly, mash the throttle pedal to the floor and when, and only when, the valve gear bursts through the bonnet, select second. Repeat the process until all the gears are used up.

A small Fiat will thank you for this, because that's what it was designed for. The original Cinquecento, the 124, the 126, the 127, the first Panda, the Uno, the Tipo, the second Cinquecento and the Seicento – they all gave of their best when they were giving of their all. You may not actually have gone very fast, but that is the Italian way – noise, drama, quite a lot of arm waving but very little actually being achieved. It was endlessly entertaining and endearing, like a waiter's arithmetic in the Lira Era.

I have a small Fiat, a Panda. I love it. The 1.2-litre engine may as well be set up to idle at 4000rpm, because using any less than that is an affront to the memory of Dante Giacosa, the man who showed us the way forward with the original Fiat 500. Drive a good one of these and you will never believe that a car is underpowered. Power per se is not the point; it is the nature of the performance that counts, and the 500 had the heart of Caruso.

This brings me to the new Fiat 500, which I've just been driving. Like the Mini and the Mustang, it leaves me a little uneasy, because I don't think pastiches of old cars work very well. The design language of the 1950s does not sit comfortably with the demands we make of a modern car; for airbags, electric windows, crash-worthiness, rollover protection, proper seats, and so on. In an original 500 it doesn't matter that the windows are so small – because you sit so close to them, and because the side of the car is only the thickness of a stout coat away from your shoulder, the bodywork impairs the vision no more than the frames of a pair of specs would. But the new one is too big for its shape and actually feels more claustrophobic as a result. Visibility is quite poor, and the chunky interior trim seems to crowd the cabin and leave it bereft of air and light.

However, I accept that this is largely a matter of fashion, and I acknowledge wholeheartedly that I am not in a position to comment on such things, as what I know about fashion could be written on the label in my brown sports jacket. In any case, the 500 is merely a Panda like mine under its shamelessly nostalgic skin, so at least it would be a hoot to drive.

Imagine my dismay, horror, abject misery, self-doubt, spiritual paralysis and even downright disappointment when I turned the key and discovered that I'd been sent the *diesel* version. I've never known an engine so ill-matched to the imagined temperament of the car to which it is fitted, and the human psyche does not admit of a demon more chilling than that conjured up by the unexpected clatter of compression ignition.

I can just about accept the dieselists' argument for Rudolf's evil invention in a large luxury car, where low-range torque can ultimately add to the sense of sophistication and calm. The petrol V8 in my old Rolls-Royce is a diesel to all intents and purposes – it redlines at 4500rpm and I've never used more than about 3500. It doesn't bother me.

But in a small car? Never. A small diesel does the job for you, but a small petrol engine demands that you enter a pact in which you must work together for the furtherance of meagre performance. The diesel grumbles and has bad breath; the petrol squeals with delight and is as fragrant as one of John Donne's mistresses. Who, in fact, could possibly even consider specifying the new Fiat 500, a car built in honour of the most under-endowed but effusive Fiat of all time, with a diesel engine? Why is this noisome instrument of the eternally tiresome even offered? Here is a spiritual sprite amongst cars, and only a serial miserablist would want it propelled by the heel-dragging drudge that is a diesel.

I know a lot of you are interested in this car. I know, too, that the diesel propaganda machine is a persuasive one. Just say no. Of course the diesel model will work out cheaper than the petrol one in the long run, but so it should. It's not as good.

And yes, there's some chance that you will melt the petrol engine, but it's all in a good cause. You'll be saving the soul of Italy.

Not to mention a large chunk of your own.

The rot stops here

Not for the first time in history, the motor industry is in a position to show the rest of commerce the way forward.

It's happened before. Henry Ford may not have actually invented mass production – we can look to the clock and gunsmithing businesses for that – but he did show that something formerly considered totally inaccessible to the normal people could actually be affordable.

In the 50s and 60s cars showed that high style and fashion could be had in an everyday consumer durable. They also encouraged the acceptance of new materials such as plastic, vinyl and even – in the door trims of the Rover P6 – Formica. More recently, and despite what the miserablists would tell you, car manufacturers have led the way in improving the dependability of the product as well as the efficiency of the means by which it is produced.

But there's still more to be done, so now I'd like to have a look at shops. When I was a small boy, shops were pretty much the way they had been since the turn of the century, which was usually closed. If they weren't closed, there was a good chance they wouldn't have what you wanted, even if it did all cost a penny.

Sadly, I'm old enough to remember the advent of the supermarket, at least up in t'north where I was living. I mean real supermarkets; huge Sainsbury's with great Babel-like towers of fruit and bog roll stretching away to eternity. I loved the supermarket when I went there with my mum to stock up for our family of six: its inconceivable inventory of stuff from all over the world, all under one roof and seemingly always open.

I still like a good supermarket, but these days it's just me and Fusker the cat, and there's the problem. It's a bit facile driving two miles to the great grocer's colossus to stand in line with my meagre basket of Whiskas and pies. A smaller, closer shop would do.

Sainsbury's realised as much, and now provides a miniature supermarket only half the distance away of the big one and probably only about a twentieth the size. Tesco have gone even further. They have really big Tescos in the wilderness, quite big Tescos on the edge of towns and town-centre Tescos called Tesco Metro. And now, at the end of my road and on the site of a former petrol station, is Tesco Local. I can almost shop there in loose robes.

But it's still not enough, because I go to Tesco, buy things, then bring them home and store them in my own cupboards. No matter how localised the supermarkets seem, there is still, in effect, an even more local one in a corner of my kitchen. Here, food goes off.

The car-making business would never allow this, because for years it has been working to the principle of 'just in time', which means that a factory carries no significant stock of parts and that all components are delivered terrifyingly close to the point in time when they will be needed.

Take Ford's Michigan Truck Plant, where its big 4x4s are assembled. An articulated lorry from a seat supplier will roll up at one door of the factory building. Its tarpaulin sides are lowered, and there, in the trailer, are enough seats for maybe three cars. They are in sets of different colours, and stacked in the correct order. They are simply loaded onto a branch of the moving assembly line and, by some miracle, end up in the right position in the right cars. This happens constantly throughout the day.

Wheels arrive at Mazda's Hofu plant in the same way. On this line, everything from a small sports car to a large panel van is made, and wheels for all of them arrive in small batches in some uncharted corner of the complex. But with minimal intervention, they all end up on the right vehicles. If it went wrong once, every car thereafter would be wrong. But it's always right, and I've never seen an MX-5 running around on the wheels from a Bongo Friendy van.

How this industrial brinkmanship is effected is one of the great mysteries of the modern world, but effected it is, and the space and overheads associated with sitting on piles of parts are saved. Once, in one of Toyota's factories, I was truly appalled at the tiny number of mounting screws available at any one time to a man whose job it was to fit headlights to Corollas. But every time I looked again, the little tub containing them had been replenished. Later in the day I discovered that I'd inadvertently put one of these screws in my pocket, and spent the night worrying that I'd brought the whole Japanese industrial engine to a shuddering and screwless halt.

Back to the local shop, where sausages are still sold in packs of six when I only want two. I buy six, and leave four in the fridge to rot. Why? Someone should hand me two sausages in the last yawning moment before I fire up the frying pan. And that gives me an idea.

I have in mind a new kitchen cupboard, one that opens into the house but also out onto the street, guarded by a simple security device. If I decide I want a fryup, I simply turn to my computer and enter exactly what I need. Ten minutes later, when I step into the kitchen and open my just-in-time cupboard, the ingredients are there: two sausages, two rashers of bacon, one egg, one piece of bread for the toast, half a tomato, two heaped teaspoonsfuls of baked beans, and a small sachet of brown sauce. How they get there I need not worry, and I need never worry that they won't be there either, just as headlight man doesn't need to fret about screw supplies.

This wouldn't be too difficult to arrange. Supermarkets already deliver, but they deliver huge piles of food that then go into a fridge, which is something Nissan would never tolerate, and rightly so. They've just come from a fridge. Why put them in another one? My scheme represents salvation for the bachelor and would free large families from the tyranny of trying to decide on Saturday what they might want to eat on the following Friday. And without the need for a fridge or all those tiresome cupboards, the kitchen can be smaller and a more agreeable room, such as the garage, a little bigger.

Apparently Honda is quite flush these days. Perhaps it could buy up Spar and set to work.

Join the police and look really stupid

Two bits of interesting reading this week. The first was an article in the *Daily Telegraph* about the future of British police transport, and the other was Mad Frankie Fraser's *Underworld History of Britain*.

On the whole, I preferred Mad Frank. I know the glorification of common criminals is supposed to be a bad thing, and I know he and his mates Cruncher and Scarface (or whatever they're called) are essentially bad men, but the trouble is that the crims come out looking a lot cooler than the rozzers. They're better paid as well, although they can only spend it in Spain.

I sense a looming crisis in police recruitment, and I'm afraid it's largely down to the image of the profession. If you're a ned, you at least get a crowbar or a knuckle duster as an entry-level badge of office, and if you turn out to be any good the firm might stretch to a dodgy drinking club in London's West End, where you'll occupy your own office with a couple of nice brasses on your desk. Join the police and you get ... well, let's take a look.

The first sign of rot was the widespread adoption of fluorescent safety-style policewear. This makes the police look a bit soft in my view, because the impression is that the personal safety of police officers is more important than pursuing the miscreant in a westerly direction and apprehending Mad Frankie in the act of doing over a pawnbrokers.

Another worrying development has been modern police

sirens. When I was a boy the Allegro patrol car had a simple blue light and emitted an authoritative bee-baa-bee-baa noise that any child could imitate. Now police cars feature the light show from a Village People concert and the whoopsie siren can only be impersonated by someone who almost got the lead role in *Some Mothers Do 'Ave 'Em*.

I'm worried that the police are being made to look a bit soft. Around here, whoever is in charge of plod has obviously been suckered into the 'branding' movement during a meeting with Bogarty Bowtie Bowtie Braces and Spectacles, and police vehicles display a legend that reads something like 'Working together in the community to raise awareness of understanding' (it's not that, but you know what I mean). I'd have 'The police – protecting you from the oiks'.

And now look – the T3 electric three-wheel vehicle. With the best will in the world, the policeman depicted riding on this thing just looks bloody silly, and you'd have no qualms about knocking his helmet off with a catapult. The boss of the company making it says the T3 has the 'wow factor', but when I look at it the sound that springs involuntarily from my lips is 'why?'

There are a few obvious drawbacks with this thing. Firstly, it has three wheels, and very few things with three wheels work properly. Secondly, you stand up to drive it. Even Karl Benz worked out that it was better to sit down.

The T3 has a top speed of 25mph, which sounds pretty good for an electric vehicle, but that's the problem. We've become so used to the dismal performance of anything battery-powered that we're impressed by even the most feeble performance figures. The fact remains that a MkII 3.8 Jag or a hooky 1600E Cortina is still a lot faster, especially in the hands of Nosher or Fingers. Yes, the T3 will mount kerbs, but so will a policeman's legs; and it won't go off road, so you don't need to be a criminal mastermind to work out which way to leg it when surprised by the bill. An electric three-wheeled vehicle is a device for allowing fat Americans to cross a shopping mall, not a front-line weapon in the fight against crime.

The sad fact is that whenever I talk to a normal bobby or traffic cop, they quickly admit that they hate all this sort of stuff. So I've come up with a much better urban police rapid response transportation system solution.

A few weeks back I bought a new Triumph Speed Triple. I was intending to have a black one, but once in the showroom I discovered that it looked very good in white, so had that instead. I think my Speed Triple has the makings of a really impressive police bike, having the power, the agility, and the correct Raffles the Gentleman Thug image to strike fear into the hearts of telly-pinching pikeys everywhere.

All they need to do is scrub out 'Triumph' on the petrol tank and substitute 'Police'. Then they need to send all the policeman to the Rocket Ron Haslam racing school, where they can learn to get it right over. Respect restored.

A postcard from France, part I

Dear readers,

I write to you from La Belle France, where I have now been for four whole days. The weather has been glorious for three of them, but very bad on the evening of the one on which we decided to camp for the night. *C'est la vie*, though normally only in the Lake District.

In case you weren't reading three weeks ago, when I was still on the Main Land, I am here for a month to make a six-part series for BBC2 on the subject of French wine. I know nothing about French wine, or indeed any other type of wine, but that's the whole point. I am accompanied by Oz 'woody finish' Clarke, the idea being that his immense and largely inaccessible knowledge of the subject will be filtered through my own ignorance and general peevishness until it is in a form palatable to normal folk who simply want a half-decent bottle of grog to knock back with the rosbif.

To that end I bought a 17-year-old Jaguar XJ-S V12 convertible, partly in the hope that it would do the decent old-Jag thing and leave me stranded in Kent, where I could just have a nice pint instead. Sadly, no. It has so far brought us all the way to Bordeaux. This is in part the fault of Knowles-Wilkins Engineering, purveyors of subtly refettled XJ-S and Series 3 Jaguars, who worked continuously on the car from the day I bought it to the evening of the day before I left.

So on this trip I have two friendships to cultivate. One with my new car, the other with Oz 'nectarine high notes' himself. And there is no better way to bond with either a car or another chap than on a proper, epic road trip.

It's a while since I drove an XJ-S. Much of it is as glorious as it ever was: the silken swelling that comes only with a full-bodied and robust petrol V12, the challenging complexity of the under-bonnet arrangement, the satisfying vintage of its green LED trip computer, and the woody finish on the dashboard.

In other ways it serves to remind us how far cars have come since this one was conceived, and convertibles in particular. The vogue for the so-called coupe-cabrio, a type of car with a solid folding roof now espoused by Vauxhall, VW, Daihatsu, Renault, Peugeot, Mercedes, Mitsubishi et al, may cause us to forget that there was a time, not so long ago, when the folded fabric roof of a large GT drophead would sit on top of the boot like the remains of the R101 airship disaster; or that the owner was expected to step outside and shroud the wreckage with an ill-fitting cloth cover that attaches by means of 1001 poppers and hooks, so that the collapsed mechanism can be disguised as a 70s sofa instead. I infer from the near-pristine condition of this 'hood bag', which takes up much valuable space in the boot, that the previous owner couldn't really be bothered. And neither, it transpires, can I.

But the old Jag is still a great car. Hopeless on the autoroute it may be – the wind wails in the gaps around the hood, the fuel consumption is atrocious, and it has the torsional rigidity of a piano accordion – but top-down on a winding D-road it has greatly endeared itself to me.

I wish I could say the same about Oz. For the last three days he has attempted to educate me in 'the vocabulary of wine' by shoving a variety of organic items – nettles, cinnamon sticks, garlic, cow poo, cashew nuts, apples, oranges, vinegar – under my nose and demanding that I 'learn' their smells. This in itself wouldn't be so bad, but all these things are now in the passenger footwell of my newly re-carpeted XJ-S, which he treats like the skip round the back of the *Ready Steady Cook* studio. *Vive la différence* is all very well, but this bloke is filling my new car with rotting fruit and spoiling the mature and musty nose of the interior. I wouldn't mind if I got a drink occasionally, but since I'm always driving I can only really commend to you the 2006 Badoit mineral water. Sparkling.

So – he gets to drink a 1988 Chateau Baron Bomburst at £75 a bottle, and I get to drive around in a 17-year-old Jaguar. Still, it could be worse. It could be the other way round.

More in a week or so.

Bon nuit,

James

The strange case of the missing Panda

A while back, I lost a pair of my trousers. Nothing too trau-matic about that – I have another pair – but what perplexes me is how this could have happened. It's perfectly easy to leave a jacket, a scarf or a hat somewhere, but trousers? That they are nowhere in the house must mean I went out with trousers on and then came home in my pants.

It gets worse. Yesterday, I went outside and discovered that my Fiat Panda was missing. That must mean I drove it to the shops, forgot I owned it and then came home on the bus. Unlikely, even by my standards.

And anyway, it wouldn't be the first time I'd lost the car. On more than one occasion I've timed a journey to the airport allowing just five minutes for stylish brinkmanship, only to open the front door and remember that, for complex reasons usually involving drink, the Panda is in the BBC car park.

But it wasn't in the BBC car park. Neither was it round the corner, and nor had it been removed by some of my 'humorous' TV colleagues. I plotted its last movements and eventually had to accept that it had been stolen. So I rang the police and took some pleasure in saying that I needed to report a missing Panda. But the woman on the other end of the phone didn't think that was funny, or even that it constituted a genuine 999 emergency, and advised me to ring the local cop shop instead. I now entered a world of hitherto unimagined woe.

First I had to ring another company to obtain something

called a 'trace' code for the vehicle for yourself sir. Then I had to give this to the police, who took details of the car and its owner and gave me a crime reference number. Then I had to give this to my insurers, who emailed a complex claim form for me to fail to print out.

And then, finally, the police rang me back to say the Panda had been located – in the local car pound. Because I hadn't paid the road tax. One of several great things about the Panda is that, as a small and economical car, its annual road fund licence is discounted to just £117.50. Unless you're me, in which case it turns out to be £420.

Now you're probably thinking rules is rules and there isn't one for me and another for everyone else. But what bothers me about this is that, as a busy man with his nose pressed to the relentless grindstone of the Protestant work ethic, who had simply committed a small oversight and of course viewed the payment of tax as a civilising duty, I was being treated no differently from a common chancer who had no intention of paying at all. That the disc was two months out of date was a mere technicality and not a basis on which to besmirch my good character.

It would be more neighbourly, I pointed out to the man in the office of whichever contractor now deals with these things, to ring or write and gently remind the blameless and law-abiding middle-class citizen of his error. That the reminder was sitting in a vast pile of post I couldn't be bothered to open is neither here nor there.

And why, I have to ask, is an untaxed but otherwise road-legal car towed away without further ado, when something like a pre-emptive fine would have spurred me into action and saved a great deal of inconvenience and expense for everyone involved? Just because the towaway truck drives around with a siren blaring to give potential offenders an even chance is not really material, and the simple fact that the car was clamped for three days during which I could have paid the road fund licence with no further questions asked is merely an attempt to fudge the issue in question, which is that I'm being unfairly criminalised for a brief lapse into human fallibility.

And here's the bit that really enrages me. Having taken my car away, they didn't even bother to tell me. It might have been weeks before I noticed. Just because they wrote to me immediately is no sort of defence. They should have realised from the way I ignored the reminder that I don't open any of this stuff.

Once again the honest, upright and accountable people of Britain are being punished as an example to a criminal fraternity that couldn't care less. The agencies of law and order, lacking the balls or authority to deal with the real blights on society, imagine we will be fooled by the odd campaign to harass the very people who could be depended upon to support them. Or something like that. Soon, we will decide we've had enough of it, and we will rise up.

In the meantime, though, it might be worth checking that your tax disc is still current.

If the car fits, wear it

When I saw it on its hanger, I thought the yellow shirt with the green lozenge pattern and contrasting embroidery looked pretty good. I like a Lego palette in casual clothing, so I tried it on.

But when I looked in the shop mirror, I had to acknowledge that I looked a bit of a berk. I was a middle-aged man in a shirt obviously designed to complement the attitude of a feckless, shuffling youth with trousers hanging around his arse and an iPod playlist to match. So I put the shirt back on the rack and bought a brown jumper instead.

This brings me to the new Maserati GT. I really like the look of that car. I'm a bit of a fan of modern Masers in general, and especially of the later V8 engine with its muscle-car crank angles and subdued yet guttural exhaust note. Where Lambos and Ferraris are for footballers and pop stars, Maseratis are somehow far more discreet and generally driven by gentlemen and ripping gals. Sophia Loren had a Maserati, and so did the Shah of Persia. I like to think of myself as a Maserati kind of bloke.

But I could be wrong, and here we arrive at a potential pitfall for the modern motorist. I bet no car showroom in the country has a mirror in it, so how can I be sure I don't look a complete knob in the GT? Furthermore, while sales assistants in clothes shops will often be honest and tell you how much better you look in the plain blue one, I suspect a Subaru dealer would sell an Impreza to a man who walked in with a white stick.

Be honest: have you ever heard a car salesman say anything like 'I'm not sure you're really quite enough of a pikey to drive this particular model, madam,' or 'If you don't mind me saying so, sir, I think your face is a bit too circular for the BMW Z coupe. You have an enduringly comedic countenance, and this is an aggressive-looking car. May I suggest a Nissan Micra?' It doesn't happen, which is why I saw that very man driving such an ill-fitting BMW only yesterday.

I know, from observing as much in a large shop window, that I look as big a pillock in a Chrysler PT Cruiser as I would in a Sari. But that's not to say that you would. All we can know for certain is that the dealer won't help in this respect, so it's up to us.

I now realise how easy it is to get this wrong. I realise because my own Porsche is obviously a bit of a case in point judging by some of the comments I've overheard from bystanders. When I bought it, I didn't think to check—the Porsche dealer doesn't have a mirror either—but now I've had a good look in the window of John Lewis while stuck in a jam I can see that, while it's not quite as ridiculous as plus fours, it might be a bit borderline for the tatty T-shirt kind of chap that I really am.

It's so very tempting to imagine that the attributes of the car will automatically be assumed by you, the potential new owner. But it simply isn't true. Porsche has an enviable sporting pedigree, a history of uncompromising excellence, and a reputation for delivering peerless quality. But that won't actually make you any less fat, blotchy, and working in the financial services sector, so you will still look like a man who shouldn't have bought a 911. There are a lot of them around, I've noticed.

So to the man in the old E-type: you're too tall and your face is too thin. You should be in a Citroën DS. To the short man in the Seat Leon: this car's waistline is high, but yours isn't. You are a reasonably good-looking bloke and your car is quite rakish. But it looks as though it's being driven by a disembodied head on a stick. And to the woman in the Mercedes E-class diesel: your hair is too mad, and someone should have had the decency to tell you how much better a Land Rover Defender would have suited you.

Style, as I believe Samuel Wesley said, is the dress of thought, so it's worth checking your appearance before you go out. The other day I saw a serious-looking besuited bloke with neat hair driving a bright green Smart car. And I couldn't help but react in the way my mother does whenever she sees a man walking bare-chested around town.

Go and put a proper car on.

Thank you for buying an unfinished car

Something that's always bothered me about the car business is this: why can't manufacturers just get the bloody car right first time around?

I'm not suggesting for a moment that Karl Benz should have realised, as he was cranking over his Motorwagen, that what he should have been doing was designing something like the C-Class and then shoehorning a 6.3-litre V8 into it. I'm talking about the way a given model supposedly 'evolves' over its lifetime.

There are countless examples of what I mean – probably as many as there are cars – but the general pattern of things goes like this. A new car is launched, and it's reasonable for us, the buyers, to assume that it's finished and as good as it can be, and that the people who designed it kept their noses pressed to the grindstone until no further opportunity for refinement of the idea could be conceived. But then, a year or two later, the maker announces that it has retuned the engine for increased low-range torque, and we in the motoring press become terribly excited about how much easier motorway overtaking has become.

Or perhaps the specification of the springs and dampers is changed to improve the ride and handling, so we all have a drive, talk to a suspension engineer for a bit and come away amazed at what they can do these days.

Or maybe some more welding points are added to the body

shell to enhance rigidity, and that's very welcome, and all part of the process of continuous improvement we've heard so much about.

But maybe a salient question is in order here, such as; why didn't you just do it like that in the first place?

It's not as if automotive engineering is a black art any more. It's a minutely understood and completely quantified science. No one with the brains to calculate that a car should run on 15-inch wheels could possibly fail to realise that it would work better on 16-inch ones, or that 180lb ft of torque is more useful if it's available at 2000rpm rather than 2500. Yet we are expected to believe that they miraculously work all this out only after 500,000 cars have been built.

A case particularly close to my heart is that of the Porsche Boxster. Two years ago, having realised that nobody fancied me any more, I decided that it was about time I owned a mid-sized two-seat roadster, and set about trying them all out to see which I liked best. Eventually, I settled on the Boxster 3.2S, for its combination of quality, driving dynamics, performance and discreet styling. It was clearly the best of the bunch, and I couldn't really fault it – beyond the rather churlish criticism that the engine was only 3.2 litres and not, say, 3.4, like it would be in the forthcoming Cayman.

A year or so later, Porsche boldly announced the 3.4S Boxster. They had shaved a little bit of metal from inside the cylinders or minutely altered the dimensions of the crankshaft and made the engine a bit more powerful. Excellent. But did they honestly expect me to accept that this was the fruit of a year's worth of scratching their egg-shaped heads and staring at a cutaway drawing of a flat-six? They must have known it was possible all along, in which case I'm forced to conclude that they deliberately sold me a car slightly less good than it could have been, and that the new and improved Boxster S was merely the one they should have given me in the first place.

Now at this point business types – the sort of people who,

at airports, pull their cabin luggage along on wheels and understand all those meaningless advertisements for the services of management consultants and the benefits of relocating to Wales – will be wanting to tell me that this is all part of keeping the market buoyant and managing customer expectations, or some such twaddle. It was once explained to me that Jaguar deliberately staggered the facelifting of its cars so that it would have something new to announce every year. But how can a car maker honestly plan a facelift? If they know the car can be made better, they should make it that way from the outset and stop wasting everyone's time and money. It would be like Gustave Eiffel designing the perfect tower but then building his first draft, just so he could return a decade later and make it look better; or a concert pianist recording a few bum notes so he could release a better version of the same CD later on.

The whole thing is a plot, obviously; the deliberate subversion of excellence in the interest of manipulating our desires and aspirations. Pah.

By the way, this column isn't quite as good as it could be. I deliberately wrote it that way so I can do it again next month, only better.

Is there a doctor in the garage?

Over the years, my local doctor has cured me of a number of minor ailments ranging from specific disorders of the bowels brought on by foreign travel to more obscure complaints such as general malaise. The only thing that has defeated her so far is my well-documented but largely unacknowledged tropical disease, which has yet to be formally recognised by medical science.

I quite like a visit to the doctor. She's a bit of a car fan, and as well as her daily driver she owns a 1980s 911 and, like most intelligent and interested people, she has a general understanding of how the thing works. But I'm pretty sure she's never picked up a spanner.

This brings me to an idea I've had for an experiment. I need a basically sound car suffering from some sort of typical but indeterminate engine malfunction, and a bloke racked with the ague but not in any way in a critical condition. A slightly poorly car and a person feeling a bit out of sorts. Then I want to give the car to a GP and the patient to a mechanic from a mainstream car business, and see who comes up with the correct diagnosis.

My money's on the doctor. And here's why. Medical training equips doctors, even non-specialists like GPs, with a scientific and analytical approach to identifying problems. Whatever training it is that car mechanics have doesn't do this. Car mechanics generally seem to guess, and just keep on replacing bits until the problem goes away, if at all.

I think the car mechanic business is facing some sort of crisis, and the problem has been generated, to some extent, by the cars themselves. A car is no longer a complex machine of many parts; it's now a collection of relatively simple machines bolted together. Sub-assemblies are invariably sealed, like those computer printers with 'no user serviceable parts inside'. If there's a problem with battery charging, they'll replace the whole alternator. And then the battery itself. And then perhaps the ECU computer and eventually the loom, or it might be the ignition switch. This wouldn't work in medicine. You'd go into the consultation room with a runny nose and come out with a face transplant.

Many dealerships, I suspect, aren't really interested in mending things at all. They're in the business of routine servicing, which I reckon has turned into an elaborate form of insurance. While your new car is under warranty, it will be honoured provided you stick to the service schedule and hand over the cash. The servicing is really simple stuff like oil changing and brake-pad replacement. Try taking a 10-year-old car with an unknown fault to a mainstream dealer, and watch them quake with terror.

As many experts will tell you, once the warranty is out you're better off with an independent, but even then you're not safe. Let's consider my good mate Colin, who has bought an old Mercedes which, obviously, went wrong within days. The man from his breakdown organisation said it was the fuel pump. The man from the local garage said it was a valve in the injection system. Someone else said it was an air leak. Eventually his wife suggested, correctly as it turned out, that there was so little fuel in the tank it wasn't getting through consistently. But imagine if he'd listened to them instead of her. He'd almost have a new engine by now when all he needed was a tenner's worth of unleaded.

Another example of this concerns my little aeroplane, the tailwheel of which went wonky so it would only steer to the right when on the ground. The sensible solution would be to pay a man to sort it out, especially as it's quite important. But hang on. The usual posse of pilots and amateur spannermen crowded round to say it needed packing with grease, that the links to the rudder pedal were too short, although they might be too long, that the retaining bolt was too tight/too loose/the wrong type, that the wheel was the wrong size. It was all bollocks, and at the end of the day visitors were still wondering why James May spent so much time taxiing around the airfield perimeter instead of just parking. I was doing this for the very reason that you would take a circuitous route from your house to the shops if your car would only turn in one direction.

See what I mean? The culture of spannering has somehow not encouraged a logical approach to analysing the problem, with the result that there are socket sets whirling around all over the country taking things apart unnecessarily and a huge business in place selling spares that aren't actually needed. And I know it worries people; people with classic cars, youths with ratty Peugeots misfiring on one, old dears with a Volvo they've had since new but that now won't start properly. What the hell are these people supposed to do?

Well, I've discovered that the best spannermen in Britain aren't actually in garages at all. They're at the National Motor Museum in Beaulieu. I was there the other day filming something for *Top Gear*, and while you may be familiar with the car collection itself, all shiny and beautifully laid out behind ropes, I am now in with the blokes in the workshop, who have to keep everything running.

Imagine what they're up against. There's over 100 years' worth of cars here, ranging from early Benzes and Renaults with ridiculous tiller steering to Grand Prix cars of the modern era. They can sort all of them, and often without the aid of off-the-shelf spares. Halfords simply do not have anything for a de Dion Bouton. The Beaulieu mechanics have to be able to mend the whole history of the motor car.

I mentioned to one of them a problem I was having with the carburettors on an old Honda motorcycle. He talked unassailable logic for about ten minutes in the manner of a scholar of Socrates, and eventually arrived at a component that I should remove, clean, and replace. I tried it when I got home and bugger me if he wasn't absolutely spot on.

There's a great business opportunity for Lord Montague here. Visit the National Motor Museum, and have your car fixed while you're there. I'm wondering if they can do anything about my cold sweats.

Trust me, I was a choirboy

There are ambitious dads everywhere who imagine that their sons will grow up to be better men if they play rugby, join the school officer cadet corps or volunteer for social work during the summer holidays.

And they probably will – up to a point. They may go on to manage banks, captain industry and generally uphold society with their yeomanlike qualities. We need people like this, so I wouldn't for a moment wish to discourage the accepted routes to the formation of good manly character. But if you want to be sure that the lad will mature into a truly redoubtable pillar of the male community, you need to put him in the church choir.

This is widely misunderstood. I hear people say things like 'Jenkins is a bloody good bloke. Winger for Chodford High you know', but this is no absolute guarantee of his dependability. If you're in a really tight spot and all hope seems to be lost, you want to be sharing the blood-spattered shell hole with a chap who once sang the solo in Samuel Sebastian Wesley's 'Blessed Be the God and Father'. He's your man.

I was a choirboy, and so were all the best people I know. It's why I turned out so well; that and being barred from watching ITV.

The choir – or, more specifically, the gaps between the weddings and other services – was the unforgiving arena in which we were made whole. Many were the couples who were eased into marital bliss at Whiston Parish Church with 'Jesu,

Joy of Man's Desiring' performed by a group of 13-year-old boys with black eyes, swollen lips, dead legs, Chinese burns and mental trauma. These were the result of severe and faintly occult rituals performed in the sanctity of the graveyard, which didn't do me any harm and went some way to making me what I am.

The only proper fight I ever had took place behind the teetering headstone of a woman who died when Victoria was a girl, was necessary to decide who would do the collection the following Saturday, and was with a boy called Kenneth, whose streaming nose remains as clear in my mind as the purity of his high Gs. And my shiner. I seem to remember that my dad gave me 50p for this performance, having recognised its significance in the formation of my character. I've no idea what happened to Kenneth in later life, but if you happen to be working with him today you can be assured that he is a man of unassailable moral fibre.

If you think choirboys are soft, you obviously never met any. You certainly didn't call our head boy a poof, otherwise you wouldn't have such a symmetrical face. As a choirboy, you were required to prove yourself; because, as a choirboy, you wore a dress.

So here comes the motoring connection, and unfortunately I've just realised it's a bit tenuous. I've been driving a BMW 530, which I think is a fine car and an interesting piece of modernist design. My criticism would usually be that it looks slightly knock-kneed. This particular one, however, was fitted with the M-Sport bodykit, which – perhaps uniquely in the history of bodykitting production cars – actually improves it. It makes the Five look very sculptural and contemporary.

But I had my reservations. Just as the cassock left me wide open to accusations of being a bit of a girl, the M-Sport BMW could be seen as a car in an aftermarket paddock jacket and might make me look a bit of a plonker. I would therefore end up driving it aggressively and discourteously just to redress the balance. As it transpired, though, I drove it like Jesus, because I was conscious that other people would assume I was a bit of a berk and was keen to prove them wrong.

I should have realised this. Occasionally I find myself driving the Range Rover we use as a *Top Gear* filming car, and because I know many people out there view a big 4x4 with utter disdain and are assuming poor moral rectitude on my part as a result, I drive like a man who's just collected a Ming vase. Put me back in the Panda and I drive like an idiot.

So if you're a fundamentally decent sort of cove – a reformed chorister, for example – do BMW, Mitsubishi, Subaru and Lamborghini a favour. Drive a rugger-bugger's sort of car. You can be relied upon to do it properly.

There you go. I told you this didn't stand up very well.

The seed of despair

I have pretty straightforward views on the business of saving fuel. Saving fuel is for fools. I don't even accept that, for some people, driving is a necessary evil, and that it should be done as cheaply as possible. Driving is not necessary at all, because trains and buses are very good these days and still cheaper in real terms. So kindly use them, and free up more road space for people like me who actually enjoy cars.

And as cars are my hobby, I can't really object to having to spend money on petrol, rather in the way that fishermen can't really object to having to buy maggots, and enthusiasts of hotel television can't reasonably object to the price of Kleenex. Given the choice between a car I'd enjoy driving and one that would save me £10, I'd always spend the extra tenner.

I even have an environmental argument in favour of thirsty cars. Everyone tells me that burning fossil fuels is a bad thing, and that it is destroying lives. In which case, surely it makes sense to buy something like an old Bentley or 60s American Muscle car and do your bit to help rid the world of this stuff. That way it won't be around to blight the lives of your grandchildren.

However, I've now changed my mind. I've changed it so much that I've sold my ageing Range Rover and bought a new 1.2-litre Fiat Panda, a car that steadfastly refuses to drop below 40mpg even if I thrash it and which, if I'm not paying attention, will readily crack 50. It saves petrol, and that's something we need to do.

We need to save petrol because the nation is in great peril. The nation is in great peril because of enthusiasm for alternative fuels. And amongst alternative fuels the most fashionable is biodiesel.

I don't like biodiesel; 'tis a silly fuel. For a start, it smells all wrong. The other day we were filming *Top Gear* near a farm where the stuff is made, and at one point the farmer went off to the bank in his biofuel-powered old Volvo. The sensation was similar to that experienced on driving past a kebab shop, only now the kebab shop seemed to be driving past me. That's confusing to an olfactory system conditioned over many decades. It's like Pavlov ringing his little bell then kicking his dog up the arse.

Unfortunately, biodiesel also smells pretty bad long before it makes it to the exhaust pipe. If I've understood *The Archers* correctly, it is made from oilseed rape, which stinks to high heaven just growing in a field. It's also an ugly yellow colour and is completely ruining the countryside, which, after all, is for driving through and admiring. England is supposed to be a green and pleasant land. I haven't given permission for it to be turned into a yellow hell that whiffs of Richard Hammond's unpleasant hair products.

It's a much bigger problem than you may have realised, driving around at ground level. I also fly light aircraft, and generally at fairly low altitude since I'm scared of heights. From 2500 feet I can see quite vividly just how much of the sceptred isle is being given over to this unutterably crap crop, and believe me it's quite a lot. The only possible benefit I can conceive of is that soon I'll finally be able to find my way back to the airfield, because it will be the only bit of the whole country that's still green.

Oilseed rape is absolutely and without question completely changing the face of our land, and for the worse. All of a sudden, the immutable Arcadian splendour that for centuries has been celebrated by our poets, artists and musicians, and which is at the heart of the rural idyll for which we all secretly yearn, looks as though it's been splattered with the sort of margarine they use in my local cafe.

Is this what we want? Do we want a hilltop view of Kent or Cumbria to look like the rejected artwork for an old Beatles album? I don't, so I'm doing my bit with a small car with a small engine that will help keep us in proper petrol for decades.

In any case, I've always liked small, simple cars with a sense of humour. The Panda is one such; immediate, efficacious, more than enough car without actually being much of one at all. It's surprisingly practical, amusing to drive and comedic in appearance. Oh, and economical, too.

Because I'm weak, I allowed the salesman to talk me out of the most basic model I'd vowed to buy and into the posh Eleganza version. But this means I have a trip computer and, at the touch of a button, can see immediately how well I'm doing in my quest to preserve what it was the poet John Clare was talking about.

You might think economy driving is boring. It is if you're simply trying to save money. But imagine the thrill that suffuses me when I see on the little dashboard display that I've saved another few acres of our island home from the yellow peril. This is something I can enjoy every day, unlike putting in a good time around Castle Combe.

There's only one problem: people have completely misinterpreted my motives. Some neighbours have imagined that I'm concerned about the difficulty in parking where I live. Others have assumed I'm taking advantage of the lower road tax for small cars. Couldn't care less. Someone even suggested that I'd caved in to public pressure about the unsuitability of big 4x4s in cities, and that I'd exchanged the old Rangey for a biffabout to ease my conscience. Not interested.

And then, the other day, I turned up at a *Top Gear* shoot

with the other two. Clarkson was driving the V8 Audi Q7,
Hammond the Honda S2000, and I was in my Panda. 'Oh,' said
a bystander. 'I'm pleased to see that one of you drives an eco-
friendly car.'

How dare he? I don't give a stuff about the eco. Or parking,
or congestion, or road tax, or fuel duty, or my carbon footprint.
Me and my Panda are engaged in something far more important.

We're saving England.

Cheese grater, plug, wheel. It's obvious

One of the few things that Jeremy Clarkson and I agree about is that the world, overall, is getting better. Traditionally, everyone over the age of forty-five believes that the place is going to hell in a handcart, but if you think about this, it can't be true. Presumably people have been saying as much since William the Conqueror arrived, and if it were actually happening we'd have got there long ago.

In truth, everything improves. Life expectancy lengthens, standards of living rise overall, more diseases are banished and people in Manchester no longer have to eat coal. I can't imagine a single aspect of plague and jester-ridden medieval life that would have been better than the one we enjoy today.

Certainly, every artefact of man's making gets better. The car certainly does, but so do things that have been with us for centuries, such as the mechanisms of wristwatches, cement and woodworking tools. Very few things have reached the peak of their development and stayed there.

But there are one or two. One that springs to mind is the mouli cheese grater, a device that allows single men to make welsh rarebit without the ends of their own fingers in it. I've studied mine very carefully and can't see how it could be improved. Better materials would make no difference, and its dimensions and simple mechanism seem to have been perfectly refined. I've had mine for twenty years and the one you buy today is exactly the same. Mouli grater – sorted.

Another is the rubber bathroom-sink plug. The French popularised the type that is shaped like a metal mushroom and operated by a lever on the tap assembly, but they never fit properly and let all the water out. My downstairs guest bathroom has a sort of silvery disc that pivots in its hole, and I knew when I bought the sink that it would leak like a government ministry. It does, and I'm often awakened early in the morning by the stream of blasphemy emanating from the half-shaved faces of visitors.

It's all very well trying to express your 'design literacy' through your choice of bathroom fittings, but sooner or later you're going to have to admit that only a rubber bung on the end of a chain is truly reliable, and stick with it. We've known it for several hundred years. Sink plug – job done.

And now to the steering wheel. As a means of steering a car, I really don't think it can be beaten. Early cars had tiller arrangements, like boats, and I believe there may have been attempts to steer them with the feet, but the steering wheel had been adopted by Benz before 1900 and even British Leyland couldn't improve on it, although they tried with that quartic nonsense.

Elsewhere, and more recently, joystick control has been tried. Saab famously came up with such a system, and it worked at an academic level, but not so well that they let anyone drive it on a real road. More recently, it has been possible to engineer in feedback with elaborate sensors and microprocessors, but what's the point? Perfect feedback can already be achieved by joining a circular wheel to the steering mechanism with solid pieces of metal, so why remove that and then try to replicate it?

The steering wheel is a perfectly logical, truly analogue triumph for the man/machine interface, and I don't believe it will ever be usurped so long as the car is with us. Steering wheel – rock on.

Imagine my dismay when I learned that some people in the

automotive engineering community now believe that cars in the future will be steered with two thumb-operated buttons, in the style of the Playboy gaming console. If, like me, you've ever wasted any of your life away on one of these things, you will know this is a stupid idea. Opposed thumbs may be what separate us from the beasts of the field, but they were not meant for steering cars.

What worries me, though, is that the first car I ever drove was a real one, on a real road. Now, however, a new generation of drivers is emerging; one that learned to drive through virtual Britain on a Gamestation. Is it possible that thumb-steer for them is as intuitive as a wheel is for me? That the steering wheel only makes sense because that's how I was nurtured? That a wheel-guided car might seem as preposterous to them as a buttock-operated Mouli grater would to me?

I don't believe it, not for a minute. But I've just realised something. By the time you read this I'll be forty-five, and the world will be going to hell in a handcart.

I'll see you there. I'll be the bloke in the small Fiat with the funny circular thing in it.

When you have finished reading, you may hang up

The following very important piece of information is intended for all those friends and colleagues of mine who insist on talking to me on integrated car telephone systems.

It is now time for us to gird our loins, brace ourselves, and admit that these things – like the Soda Stream machine, buttoneer and toasted sandwich maker before them – number among those devices that endure for a while on the back of our fervent belief that they will be useful but in reality DO NOT BLOODY WELL WORK.

Consider the latest Mercedes E-class. I believe there was some disquiet surrounding the integrated telephone arrangement in the Command system of this car, because by the time it was launched the type of blue-toothed telephone solution required for its correct operation was no longer available. I gather that some owners are pretty sore about this, but they needn't be. It wouldn't have worked anyway.

I've had it up to here with people pretending to talk to me on built-in car phones. Jeremy Clarkson, for example, who remains convinced that every other telephone in the world is malfunctioning and cannot accept that the one supposedly incorporated in his SLK is about as useful as a speed hump on an airfield runway. I'm straining so hard to hear him that soon those minute bones in my ear, the ones that receive sound waves, will be on the outside of my head.

Only the other day, he rang me from the car and said, I think, that he had something very important to ask me. Whatever it was, I probably agreed to it. I have conducted whole conversations with him during which I've responded generically with 'yes', 'gosh' and 'ha ha ha' when he might have said something amusing, but in reality I haven't heard from the bloke in ages.

Not to be outdone, my other colleague, Richard Hammond, has had something similar fitted to his Porsche. Whenever he rings me, bored, on a car journey, I tell him to speak up because I can't hear him properly. He then regales me with an anecdote that would no doubt be quite entertaining delivered in measured tones in the warm confines of a local pub, but which loses something in a declamatory presentation style that conjures up an image of him turning more purple in the face as he bawls his way to the punchline. It's like listening to Windsor Davies read Psalm 23 in his *Ain't Half Hot* voice.

One day, out of interest, we spent a good half an hour scouring the cabin of the Porsche in search of the exact location of the little microphone that must be in there somewhere. It was nowhere to be found. The next time he rang, I realised we'd made a mistake in assuming it was *inside* the car. It's clearly up the exhaust pipe or inside one of the cylinders.

There's more. An important executive I know, the head of a very go-ahead company, often rings me from his car. The other day, he may have offered me some very lucrative work. Sadly, I'll never know.

What is to be done? Tricky. One friend found a way around the whole phones-in-cars law simply by Sellotaping his existing mobile to the centre of the steering wheel. I can hear him perfectly well, but now I have to shout to bridge the yawning three-foot chasm between the tinny carpiece and his actual ear.

And, as we know, one cannot use one of those wireless ear attachment things because one will end up looking like a bodyguard, someone in the early throes of elephantiasis or, worst of all, a plain berk.

The answer, I believe, is to return to those long earpieces-on-a-string that everyone was using a few years ago. These work and they're legal, but unfortunately they reintroduce another phobia of mine – crinkly wires.

Crinkly wires are hideous and everywhere these days: on computers, on satnavs, on home cinema systems, and on the 101 little plug-in transformers we need for recharging rechargeable things. They're the ruin of England.

So what I propose is a normal mobile phone with a long wire that retracts into its body at the press of a button, like one of those extending leads that people with very small dogs have. I've mentioned it to a nice man who works for the Carphone Warehouse.

And we know how successful my inventions are.

Citroën Ooh La La

A problem I'm feeling more acutely than ever these days is that there's a whole band of the motoring spectrum (sorry, been talking to some marketing people) that leaves me completely cold.

Luxury cars I've always loved: Rollers, Bentleys, old Cadillacs, anything unashamedly indulgent. I like supercars for their comedy value and true sports cars for the pleasures to be had at the man/machine interface. I've also had a lifelong love of truly simple small stuff – my peerless Panda, an original Mini, even the likes of the Perodua Kelisa.

But that leaves a lot of cars in the middle, and this is where I have some difficulty. I simply don't know what to make of a small MPV or lifestyle 4x4 soft-roader. The Vauxhall Zafira is clearly quite clever and the Toyota Rav4 is doubtless a pretty good car, but neither of them blows my frock up in any way. Same goes for a mid-size estate or a popular family hatch remodelled as a coupe cabrio with a metal folding roof.

Worst of all, though, is the spectre of the so-called executive car. I have to be truly honest here – I'm bored to death with Audi, BMW and Mercedes saloons. They are po-faced and humourless, even when they come with big engines and more knobs than the Radio 1 mixing desk. I can't drive an Audi A6 or 5 series without thinking I'm involved in something blue-chip and solutions-driven through the use of enabling technologies. I'm convinced that the people who drive these things use the word 'logistics' a lot.

I have therefore become a champion of the Citroën C6, which I have just driven to France and back with my new chum Oz 'Alka-Seltzer' Clarke, who was the bloke on the *Food and Drink* show back in the days when the television was a very large wooden box with a very small screen in the middle. So intrinsically 'right' was the combination of alternative French car and evidently British driver that I made it on and off the ferry and into Calais without a passport. I even made it back without having to pass a Britishness Test, although they did take me to one side to check the boot for Albanians. Maybe they'd heard how big it is.

At this point, I could easily slip into the usual drivel that accompanies any analysis of what is generally considered one of the most perilous purchases available to motoring man, i.e. a big French car. This would include a quote from Roland Barthes (a big fan of the original DS); something about intellectualism, cafe society, cheese, revolutionary tendencies, égalité and so on. What I really like about the big Citroën, though, is that it's so adamantly unfashionable. Here is a car that has never even heard of the Nürburgring. It flops into corners, and over a gentle undulation it performs a trick that only an old Rolls-Royce Corniche can match; that of appearing to remain suspended in space for a second or so before sinking back to earth. This, the shape of the rear window and the funky 70s-style door bins pretty much sell the whole car to me.

I can see that it's not perfect. The ride would be even better if Citroën had not fallen foul of the vogue for large wheels with low-profile tyres. A luxury car should have it the other way around, so that the tyres alone can absorb small ridges without bothering the whole suspension. My mum understands this perfectly well. The head-up display, which presents a digital speed reading apparently floating above the road somewhere in front of the car, is spoiled under certain light conditions, when the surround of the dash-mounted projector is also reflected in the screen. It's like that moment at an illusionist's theatre show when the mirror is inadvertently revealed behind a curtain.

And there are little things. The boot lid makes a rather insubstantial French noise when it shuts and, as has been true of every big Citroën since 1955, the engine doesn't seem quite big enough. The interior is also a bit conventional for a true Citroën: things such as the indicators and the ventilation controls are exactly where you'd expect them to be, whereas on a CX finding these things could provide a lifetime of on-road amusement.

But it's still great, a proper French barge that farts in the general direction of anything to do with handling or responsiveness. Better still, it managed something that my old XJ-S, even over a whole month of driving around France with the woody high-notes bloke, could never quite do for me.

Deep into a seemingly interminable monologue about the meaning of 'terroir' and the cigar-box scents of the velvety 1990 Bordeaux he'd just bought, the C6 – mercifully – sent him to sleep.

A postcard from France, part II

Dear readers,

Still having a super time here in France. The old XJ-S is going well, save for a small oil leak which I have traced – while firmly believing old cars to have a sense of irony – to the oil pressure sender unit at the back of the engine block.

This wouldn't be so bad on any other car, and would qualify as a running roadside repair at a small local garage. However, this is France, where all small local garages are characterised by being shut, and it's a V12 Jaguar, on which the oil pressure sender unit is about as accessible as the Queen's bedroom. The impression, upon looking under the bonnet, is that Jaguar's engineers placed the sender unit on a bench and then built the rest of the car around it.

None of this means anything to Oz 'hmm, fruit' Clarke, who can't believe that modern cars don't have carburettors and don't need to be decoked every winter. His only contribution to solving the problem is to observe that the smell of fresh 20/50 semi-synthetic landing on a hot exhaust pipe featured in one of his tasting notes for the 1988 Bordeaux Chateau La-La Land. We're talking here of a man who refers to the alloy wheels on his BMW as 'hub caps'.

It's quite refreshing to have travelled 1600 miles so far with a man who knows so little about cars, and whom I can bore to blazes with trivia about, for example, why the Citroën 2CV and VW Beetle are so different, despite being conceived around the same time in neighbouring countries and for essentially the same purpose; that is, mobilising The People. Well, he did ask.

In my opinion it was all about national ambition. The 2CV was designed to be capable of driving across a ploughed field, allegedly without breaking a basket of eggs placed on the passenger's seat. It was a true peasant's car, the product of a fiercely rural economy, designed to be repaired by people with access to little more than a brick and a piece of string. The engine was ruthlessly simplified, and the body-work came off so it could be beaten back into shape after witless rustics, half cut on the evil grog they still brew in sheds around here, drove into each other.

But the Beetle, while still a car for the Volk, was conceived by the Führer for the new *Autobahnen*, and especially the dead-straight one he envisaged running from Berlin to Moscow. Like most German machinery of the 1930s, it made the transformation to military equipment suspiciously easily. The Beetle formed the basis of the Kubelwagen and the Schwimwagen, in the way that Dornier's so-called 'fast mail planes' became curiously effective bombers.

This is the sort of thing I'm using to bore Oz Clarke to sleep in the passenger seat, thus preventing him from talking about the woody high notes and the long herbal finish. The flipside is that if I've had a drink and he's driving, I have to attempt to grab forty winks while he points to some desperate-looking rock-strewn vineyard and says something like 'Look at the terrain. You'll be able to taste the struggle of the vines and the wind from the hills in the 1995 Comtesse de Bomburg.'

The fact is that we're both nerds, but enthusiasts are always good company even if their subject is largely impene-trable. There's always common ground, too, and ours came in a drive across the Corbières Mountains.

The west side of the range is bad for vines. The rainfall is

high, the soil is too fertile and has too much clay in it. It's
heavily forested. Vines like harsh climates and poor ground;
even the Romans knew that 'The vine shall not go where the
wheat can grow'.

But we both agreed that it would be great in an old Mini.
The road is very narrow, little more than a tarred track, and
twists hideously. Huge power would be an irrelevance. A
Mini would skip, goatlike, from bump to bump, and rasp on
the short straights between the blind bends. The Jaguar was
wasted on it.

The east side is completely different. It takes more heat
from the sun, and the wind blows harder. It's much drier,
and the ground is rockier. The vine strives for nourishment
and gives us the aggressive red Carignan, Grenache and
Syrah grapes, renowned for their heat and high notes of
herbs and spices (says Oz).

And now the road is broader, more modern, and features
longer straights between bends that sweep rather than twist,
and where one can give it the grapes in complete safety. It's
evolved that way to serve the hardy vintner in his van, but
would also make the ideal accompaniment to a Porsche 911
3.2 Carrera like mine, or the one Oz once owned.

And that, we decided, was a good enough reason for
drinking the local Fitou.

Dogs should be able to buy their own biscuits

I've always believed that animals are much cleverer than they let on; that sheep, for example, are actually great philosophers. What else can they be doing all day? They only stand in the road in Derbyshire so we don't realise.

Consider dogs. Dog owners are always inordinately proud if the pooch can open a door or recognise the sound of its master's voice down the megaphone of an old record player, but will not admit that most things apart from a simple stick-fetching or postman-biting stunt is beyond the witless beast.

However, I reckon that's what dogs want us to think. Occasionally, a dog accidentally reveals just how intelligent it really is. When I was a small boy we had one that, of its own volition, would go and collect my big sister from school, and even knew when it was the weekend and not to bother.

In fact, it could be that dogs are canny enough to realise that if the true extent of their capabilities become known, they will have to find jobs, open bank accounts and stand around the office water dispenser discussing the value of their kennels. What dog in its right mind would actually want that? As a dog you merely have to lift a paw to earn a good square meal, and as long as you fool humans into believing you're stupid you can continue to headbutt them in the crotch for a laugh, and get away with it.

This brings me to the subject of robotic cars. The idea has been around at least since I was a lad, when it was imagined that cars would run around autonomously, guided by networks of wires hidden in the road. I seem to remember VW experimenting with just such a system. Now, of course, the whole business is much easier. Satnav can know a car's exact position in time and space, and the type of sensor that allegedly allows the Lexus LS430 to park itself can be used to detect and avoid unexpected obstacles. The self-driving car is a technical reality, and as much has recently been demonstrated in California, where a competition to design a robotic car saw the winning entry cover sixty miles in an urban environment without hitting anything. But now we arrive at a problem.

Until the robot car can somehow be programmed to pick up the paper from the newsagents, it's a bit of a red herring. There is no pleasure to be gained from sending the car off for a nice drive on its own. For a while I might be amazed at the way it disappears out of sight down the road and then returns later in the day unscathed, but no more than I am when Fusker the cat does it (who, in any case, spends most of his time in the local pub pretending to sleep on a chair when really he's working on the libretto for his new opera).

This brings me back to dogs. Dogs can already fetch the newspaper and have been doing so, at least in the *Beano*, for generations. The dog could be sent off in the robotic car to pick up the *Telegraph* and other basic provisions, so long as you provide it with a list for the shopkeeper.

But perhaps we could be a bit more ambitious about this. I reckon dogs would like driving. The animal lobby will now dismiss this as cruel and immoral, but hang on a minute. Is it any worse than making a dog work for its living on a farm or at the gate of a scrapyard? It would certainly be more rewarding for the poor mutts. Furthermore, I've never met a dog that (who?) isn't a car enthusiast. Dogs bark at cars, chase cars, urinate on cars, like being in cars and like sticking their heads out of the windows of cars. It's only natural that dogs should want to learn to drive.

And I reckon they could do it. Spatial perception is very good in dogs. They can round up sheep, catch balls and jump over fences. Steering might be an issue, as they have no thumbs, but it must be possible, using modern electronics, to devise a steer-by-wire system based on head movement, so that the car simply goes where the dog looks. That, you're going to point out, will mean straight into a lamp-post or a lady dog. Again, that may just be what they want you to believe. Everything else – brakes, gearchange, starting, door handles – can be operated via pedals. Dogs have got four legs.

I'd like a dog that could drive for me. In fact it's time they did something useful instead of just sitting around in front of the fire all day and treating the place like a hotel.

Fido has had it easy for long enough.

The incredible disappearing road

I know you've all been waiting. So here, then, reproduced entirely without permission, is some official blurb concerning the government's *Manual for Streets*, which appears to be some sort of initiative aimed at improving the design of our, um, streets. Ready? Comfortable? Here we go.

> *The purpose of the* Manual for Streets *is to consolidate the necessary components for effective street design into a single integrated source of information and guidance that will facilitate professional communication and understanding.*

There's more!

> *The manual will recognise the full range of design criteria necessary for the delivery of multi-functional streets and ensure that practitioners have the most up to date information available on the considerations relevant to those criteria, including quantitative thresholds where appropriate.*

Now. Is it just me, or is this bollocks? Having already suffered the words 'facilitate' and 'delivery', I decided I'd rather kill myself than read any more about the *Manual for Streets*. But then I realised there hadn't been a 'solution' yet, so I decided not to kill myself and to make an effort instead. And I discovered some very disturbing things about the quest to make streets 'social places, not just traffic spaces'.

For a start, I'm always deeply suspicious of any attempt by the authorities to tell me how to enjoy myself. It's all a bit Strength Through Joy for my liking. It's a small step from here to morning exercise in the park and community singing, you mark my words.

But I do agree with the basic premise that streets should be social places. In fact, the street where I live already is one. People live on it, run in and out of each others' houses to borrow a cup of sugar, grow plants, talk rubbish, and moan about the bin men. We cook meals for each other, help each other with small DIY tasks and the subsequent rush to hospital, recommend builders and ask each other politely to turn the radio down. All this happens on my street. We even drive up and down it occasionally, although if other people drive up and down it too fast, we go out and shout at them. Multi-functional? We're already there, although we haven't yet used it as a landing strip.

How could this be improved? Well, apparently, speed humps could be removed – hoorah! – in favour of a doctrine of 'shared space'. But hang on. Surely they're not suggesting that there should be no delineation between the bit generally occupied by the cars and the bit that people walk on? My own experience of ignoring this well-established divide – when crossing the road, for example – suggests that this is a good way to get run over.

But I'm afraid that's exactly what they are suggesting. In the future, the road and the pavement will be on the same level, and trees will be planted at the edge of the road bit to 'slow cars down'. I don't think this will work. I was going to ring and ask Marc Bolan, but then I remembered that he died some time ago when his car hit a tree at the side of the road.

The authors of 'Manual' have been inspired by some

residential areas in places like Holland, where the street is essentially a children's playground and cars are slowed to walking pace and, at times, even excluded completely. This won't work in Britain, though, because our children won't play in the street. They're all too fat, apparently, from spending too long slumped on the sofa watching *Lazytown*.

Elsewhere, the *Manual for Streets* suggests the construction of something called 'pocket parks' – small grassy areas near roads to encourage socialising. Again, I'm not convinced. Roads tend to be noisy, and unless you're one of those mad French people who sits in a camping chair on the verge and watches cars all day, I don't think roadsides are very sociable places. There's a good reason why a mews house in London's West End is worth £4 million and one next to the A4 is generally boarded up.

More to the point, there's something a bit like a pocket park around the corner from my house; an area with benches and a cluster of trees. It is not used for socialising. It is used by tramps drinking Special Brew. We're all socialising in the pub, and won't give any money to the tramps because they'll only spend it on drink.

Admittedly, a lot of the thinking in the *Manual for Streets* is aimed at new streets; the streets that will need to be built around the hundreds of thousands of new houses that are needed to house all those people who are currently living in boxes. Or Latvia. But there is a perfectly good model for the successful development of new streets already in place in Britain – old streets. My own street was here for several hundred years before the car was invented, but seems to be able to accommodate it pretty well. The cars go down the bit in the middle, the people go along the bits at each side, and the bin lorry reverses into my wall. Simple.

Some of the thinking in the Manual just doesn't add up. One-way streets, for example, have fallen out of favour because, apparently, they 'encourage speeding, prolonging journey times'.

Exactly how going faster makes a journey take longer is not clear, but I'd be very interested to know, not least because it would render the life's work of Isaac Newton useless.

But here's where it turns sinister. From now on, T-junctions will be deliberately designed with sharp corners so that the approach to them will be blind. This will slow cars down.

I'm reminded of a project called something like 'Towns in Bloom' that ran when I first started driving. It encouraged, among other things, the planting of great beds of flowers in the central reservations of dual carriageways, especially at the point where they broadened on the approach to a roundabout. This looked great, but the roundabout was always hidden behind a huge wall of chlamydias. So you could slow right down and have a look first, or carry on at normal speed and hope to jink around circulating traffic at the last moment. The choice was congestion or death.

And now we have a similar plan to make junctions dangerous in the interests of road safety. The government will get you on a bicycle yet. Or kill you in the attempt.

What Audi could learn from Jesus

I know everyone is terribly excited about the new Audi R8, but every time I look at it I can't help thinking it's not quite right. It's all very well from the nose all the way to the rear edge of the doors, but then ... what is it? Too long? A bit too broad? Whatever it is, its makers have drawn attention to it by painting that bit of it black.

In fact, I know exactly what's gone wrong here, and by way of explanation I would like to turn to a figurine of Jesus that I recently acquired in an exchange of plastic novelty items with our saviour here on earth, Jeremy Clarkson. No point leaving the light of the world with that miserable sinner, because He'd end up in the back of a dark cupboard. I quite like having the old Nazarene around, so Jesus is currently brightening up a shelf in my kitchen.

Usually, my first reaction on considering this sort of thing is to conclude that Islam had the right idea in forbidding all depictions of the prophet Mohammed, thus saving its popular culture from a tidal wave of ecclesiastical tat. Consider the Mezquita in Cordoba, Andalucia; a great sprawling edifice that started life as a mosque but was later turned into a cathedral. The surviving mosque part is elegant, austere, dim, and altogether conducive to deeper thought. The church bit is gaudy to the point of revulsion, and includes a statue of the Virgin dressed as if preparing for an appearance in the popular celebrity trash mag *Halo!*.

But as Jesus nick-nacks go, mine's not that bad. He's dressed in a simple shift and sash, and shod with a pair of convincingly miniaturised Desert Dockers. His arms and legs are fully jointed, so he can be posed in attitudes ranging from the contemplative to the ecstatic. His torso incorporates a small electronic voicebox thing, so when you press a hidden button in the small of His back He delivers an uplifting Gospel quotation.

Never mind that, despite what William Blake told us, the Christ child seems to have spent some time on the east coast of America, or that he was miraculously conceived in China. Curious visitors to the May household will often pick up my Jesus, unwittingly press the voice button, and be reminded to love their neighbours. So Jesus of Hammersmith is fulfilling a useful civic function as well as a purely decorative one, and if I were the local Councillor Wonderful being interviewed on the radio, I could reasonably add 'in the community'.

Last night, Fusker the cat toppled the injection-moulded Prince of Peace from his position on a high shelf, causing his sacred head to come off, though without sustaining any permanent wounds. As I pushed it back into place, I noticed something odd. Jesus's head is a very different colour from Jesus's body.

Then I noticed something else odd. Jesus's body is blessed with most steroidally inflated pectorals and biceps ever to adorn a man who turned the other cheek. He didn't get those from helping Joseph in the carpentry shop, or just from overturning the odd money-lender's table. And what's with the gripping hands? They'd be great for holding, say, a machine gun, or for allowing Action Jesus to abseil down a rope, or even for helping him grasp the paddle of a miniature canoe. The only thing his hands aren't good for is being reformed into an attitude of prayer. They always spring back into the attitude of someone about to strangle the little children.

I know what's happened here. Someone who will not enter the kingdom of heaven has taken an existing action figure, substituted a vaguely Jesus-like head, incorporated a few out-of-copyright biblical passages and then dressed the whole thing in the garb of a poor Galilean in the hope that no one will notice. And then charged £35 for it. This is not an honest and heartfelt piece of Christian iconography at all. It's a Teenage Mutant Ninja Jesus, a craven image and, to my mind, blasphemous.

Here, then, is the problem with the Audi. I know they keep wittering on about how much they've modified the weight distribution, and I know it has a different engine, but in the end it's based on the Lamborghini Gallardo, which was designed as a Lamborghini Gallardo and looks better as one. I know platform sharing is supposed to be the saviour of car design, but this platform only seems to work in its original incarnation and won't tolerate a second coming. It just doesn't quite work.

You may as well try to pass a Camel Trophy Land Rover through the eye of a needle.

Maxing the Veyron – a piece of cake

You may have seen a short film on BBC 2's *Top Gear* in which it was my mission to verify Bugatti's claim that the maximum speed of its Veyron is a genuine 253mph.

And let me say straight away that it isn't. More careful calculation in the comfort of my office reveals that the 407kmh confirmed by the on-board telemetry actually equates to 252.9098mph. We knew that car makers lied about performance figures in the 60s and 70s, and we thought that sort of deceit was a thing of the past; but here we are in 2007, and even one of the world's most respected automotive operations can't resist adding a wantonly optimistic 0.0902mph to its latest car's top whack.

Still: it's quite quick, and ever since that day I've been seeking the one word that perfectly describes what it's like to drive a car at that sort of speed; at almost 100mph more than the agreed limited maximum for German super saloons. The disparity certainly feels greater than that, at least judging by the rate at which the armco and trackside trees sped past. It's a bit noisy, too, and the banking at the far end of Ehra's five-and-a-half-mile straight loomed very large very suddenly. When I looked, the needle was pointing at a number I've never seen on a car's speedo before. But despite all this, there is a word for it. And the word is: easy.

Sorry and all that. I could big it up and would probably get away with it. Only a select few have maxed a Veyron – the

company keeps a record of their names in a little book, apparently – and no F1 car goes faster. There are but a few dozen
people in the world who have been this fast in a car, so I could
walk in to the pub and claim it as an act of heroism, safe in
the knowledge that the next quickest bloke there would be the
one who'd done 150 in his Fiesta diesel.

But, like him, I'd be lying. It's a piece of cake. You come off
the banking, floor it, change up, and wait for the 'top speed'
legend to appear in the dashboard display. The magnitude of
the Bugatti engineers' achievement is not evinced by the
absolutes of its performance figures, but by the impression that,
at its top speed, the Veyron feels as though it's performing at
two-thirds of its capabilities.

And yet – I don't believe I will ever go faster in a car. That
there will ever be a faster car to go in is in some doubt. I know
that aerodynamic drag is the issue, and that the drag increases
as the square of the velocity. I also know that the power needed
to overcome it is proportional to the drag times the velocity;
i.e. the velocity cubed. I've therefore calculated, using amateur
physics (and this is an open invitation to the usual assortment
of engineers and science teachers to write in and correct me,
with the aid of a graph), that merely to take the Veyron to
270mph will require an extra 215bhp.

That someone might build a car engine with 1215bhp, reliable enough to be used around town as well as at 270mph, is
not inconceivable. But where am I going to drive this thing?
There are some straight sections of *Autobahn* longer than Ehra's
5.5 miles, but they're rarely deserted. The 100-mile straight
running across Australia's Nullarbor Plain sounds promising,
but a stray kangaroo struck at 270mph is going to assume the
solidity of Uluru. In any case, last time I was there the local
rozzers got pretty shirty with me for doing 90.

No, I really do believe we've peaked with the Veyron. I
know we said that about the rash of 200mph supercars that
emerged in the early 90s, but this is different. The global road

map simply will not admit of a higher speed, so that's the end of that.

And it troubles me. I've driven other cars at or close to their maximum speeds, and it's always been deliciously disconcerting. The Bentley Continental Flying Spur felt commendably stable at 190, but I can't pretend I was completely relaxed. The 1991 911 RS seemed to confirm the bar-room belief that any air-cooled Porsche was designed to kill you the instant you lowered your guard, and at an indicated 110 in my 1967 Triumph Vitesse the driver's door fell off.

But here is Bugatti, with its tiresome devotion to engineering excellence, ensuring that the highest speed I will ever attain on land will also be remembered as the least dramatic. They dumped me in the rarefied environment of 252.9098mph and left me wondering if I should put the radio on.

Bloody Germans. They always have to spoil everything.

The double-ended sword of motoring progress

I accept that my push-me-pull-you double-headed Alfa Romeo cum Saab interior themed limousine is still in need of some development work, but I don't think it should yet be dismissed quite so readily as it has been by some.

If you weren't watching, this was yet another *Top Gear* project vehicle, this time in response to a challenge to each make our own stretched car. It hadn't escaped our notice that every other one we'd seen was based around something predictably American, usually a Lincoln or, in cases of extreme chavity, a Hummer. This is all very well if you really are on a hen party, but it means the stretch limo can never be elevated to a more dignified role. Tony Blair couldn't, for example, use one to travel to an international summit, because everyone would expect him to climb out wearing no knickers and covered in ladysick.

No, for the stretch limo to become acceptable, it would have to spring from something more modest and European. So Hammond bought an MG-F, Clarkson found an old Fiat Panda, and I bought two cars – a Saab 9000 and an Alfa Romeo 164, both with 3.0-litre V6 engines. Nowhere in the British Constitution does it state that the two ends of a limo have to come from the same car.

Once I'd sawn the back off both, I also realised that there was no law stating that the limo must have a bonnet at one end and a boot at t'other. So I had some blokes weld the Alfa and Saab back to back to create the beast with two fronts. It's not a completely new idea: diesel and electric railway loco-motives have always been like this, and at their advent this attribute of double-endedness was seen as a great leap forwards. In both directions.

The advantages of this layout are so manifold I can't believe no one's thought of it before. Delivering your client to the end of a narrow street? Wave goodbye to limo-manoeuvring misery by simply climbing into the other end and reversing out forwards.

So far, limo drivers have been forced to avoid the narrow Victorian streets of cities such as Manchester and London, but not in the Salfa Romeab. On approaching a tight corner, simply ask your passenger or a member of the public to climb into the end you're not in and turn the wheel the opposite way. This car[s] has a tighter turning circle than my Porsche, although the Porsche doesn't sideswipe unsuspecting newspaper vendors and orange sellers from the pavement.

Similarly, by turning the other steering wheel in the same direction, the Salfa can be made to crab around obstacles such as parked vans. Honda championed this type of four-wheel steering years ago, but never really went far enough. The rear wheels only swivelled by a few degrees, and they entrusted the control of them to a witless computer. A man who has just walked out of a newsagents does a much better job.

Admittedly, there are one or two administrative problems. Insurance is difficult, because this is technically two cars. The engine is a 6.0-litre W12 with a bit of a gap in the middle. Try explaining this to a call centre in Karachi and expecting them to quote you happy.

Furthermore, since the tax disc must be displayed in the windscreen and must denote the make of car, and as this car has two windscreens and two identities, it must be taxed twice. But there are savings to make elsewhere.

Confronted with an illegally parked Salfa Romeab, the warden must declare on the ticket what type of car it is. If he concludes that it's a Saab, I can contest the fine on the basis that I have an Alfa, and vice versa. A policeman who asks 'is this your car sir?' will be compelled to state which car he's talking about. It doesn't matter which he chooses, because I can simply claim to be in the other one.

Best of all, though, is that this radical car is the perfect foil to the London congestion charge and all the other similar schemes under consideration. For the purposes of gaining type approval, the car is a Saab. Legally, the Saab is the front and the Alfa is the back. So it is registered as a Saab, wears the Saab's number at both ends, and appears on DVLA records as a Saab. But I can drive it into London without paying a penny. The automated charging system will show that a Saab 9000 has entered the congestion zone without buying a ticket, but when the photographic evidence is checked, Ken Livingstone will see only an Alfa Romeo reversing into the city.

I'll see him in court.

Mercedes-Benz forever

One of the few things motoring journalists can't tell you about a new car is how well made it is. Obviously, we can rattle on about the noise the door makes when it shuts, and lament excess shininess on the dashboard plastics, but none of this will tell you how well the thing will be hanging together in ten years' time.

On re-reading launch reports of the Triumph Stag, for example (no, really), I find nothing to say that this car will be prone to overheating and cylinder-head gasket failure. More recently, I didn't spot in my detailed examination of the then-new Alfa 156 that the minor electrical connections weren't up to much. And no one realised that the Peugeot 205 GTi would snap its cam belts and consume its own engine if you were unlucky. It was left to owners to discover this sort of thing the hard way.

The only way to tell how well a car was mantled in the first place is to dismantle it again, and the only person to have done this with any regularity was the man whose name shall be called manual, i.e. John Haynes. For the rest of us, turning up at a swanky car-launch venue with a trolley jack, two axle stands and a 99-piece socket set tends to arouse suspicion.

Still, about twenty years too late, I have just disassembled a substantial part of a 1985 Mercedes W123, the E-class before the one before the last one. People who mend old cars have told me before that this Mercedes was one of the best-built cars in history. It harks from a time when Mercedes avowedly over-engineered everything, when the customer paid a premium for that and was rewarded with a monastic interior and wind-up windows. You bought one of these Mercs if you enjoyed the nagging suspicion that everything, including the bits you couldn't see, had been done properly.

I can now confirm that it was. Taking the old E-class apart was a lengthy and baffling exercise, because there was always another hidden bolt, another screw, another fiendishly recalci-trant clip. The glovebox lid, for example, would not yield even to Jeremy Clarkson and his Cotswolds Screwdriver*; it would come off only by reversing the process by which it was attached in the first place. In isolation, it seems like an unnecessarily complex one, but time has proved it to be unbelievably fit for purpose.

So yes, the W123 E-class was a superbly well-made artefact on a par with some cathedrals, and it has got me thinking. I now know what old people are on about when they lament the passing of the mendable appliance. This week I have been forced by manufacturing timidity into discarding a kettle, a toaster, and a pair of binoculars. The kettle leaked, the toaster suffered a simple internal electrical failure, and the binoculars had water in them, but as none of them had been built to be rebuilt one day there was nothing I could do about it. Dualit toasters and the Rowlett model I have bought, for all their knowing ponciness, are held together with self-tapping screws and other things that can be removed and replaced endlessly. Like the yard broom of two-heads-and-three-handles fame, they are infinitely repairable.

Because the Mercedes was built properly, it came apart prop-erly. And because it came apart properly, it would go back together again. No doubt in the twenty-two years that my example had roamed the earth quite a few parts had been

---

*Hammer

replaced – it certainly didn't have its original gearbox, and various small components were obviously of newer vintage. But somebody once told me that only half of Westminster Abbey is the original building. So what? It's still Westminster Abbey. Whoever engineered my Mercedes must have wanted it to last for a very long time.

This is, I suspect, an increasingly unfashionable approach to making anything in large volumes. Sooner or later, and as with the kettle, the toaster, the laser printer and the washing machine, the car, even a superbly made one, crashes headlong into the argument about economic viability. But why? We drive around in a car for maybe ten or fifteen years, then decide we're bored with it or it's somehow not worth maintaining any more. So we throw it away – the whole car!

But look at the life of a typical W123 Mercedes like mine. It enjoyed what we would think of as a full life in the west before starting a new one as a taxi in the developing world, after which it began yet another existence in the hands of a private owner with the odometer already indicating a trip to the moon.

There is no reason why it shouldn't last until the end of time.

One good thing came out of the 1970s

I don't know if Santa has kept my letter dated December 1977, but if he has, he'll be distressed to know that I haven't changed my mind.

I was terribly grateful for the Airfix Avro Lancaster and the Top Trumps supercars pack, and I could even summon up a wry grin at the efforts of some misguided relation to help spur me through adolescence with a bottle of Boots Satinwood after-shave (I still have it, unopened). But these were a sorry substitute for that thing the mere thought of which was keeping me awake until dawn.

I was just a perfectly normal teenage boy in 1977; by day gazing wistfully out of the window during 'Naming of Parts', by night driven to dementia by unsated lust. All I wanted was to get my leg over the Yamaha FS1-E sports moped.

Surely you remember the Yammy Fizzie? The Fizzie was the world's best example of marketing opportunism in the face of a legislative loophole. The minimum legal age for a proper motorcycle was 17, but for years the British had been fitting small clip-on auxiliary petrol engines to conventional bicycles. My dad did this. Eventually, the fashion was framed by legislation that said a moped – the word is a contraction of MOtor-assisted PEDal-cycle – could be ridden at 16 provided it retained its pedals and the engine capacity was under 50cc.

And there it might all have ended, with history recording the ultimate expression of the moped as the French Velosolex or the similar machine, made by Raleigh, whose name now eludes me. At best it was a step-through such as the Motobecane or Puch Maxi. But right at the point when the rulebook was dusty with neglect, the Japanese motorcycle giants, plus a few Italians, recognised that they could snare their prospective customer base a full year earlier simply by building a high-performance 50cc bike and taking the expedient step of equipping it with nominal pedals.

This may not sound like much of a sales initiative by modern standards, but put yourself in the mindset of a 16-year-old, to whom the year that must pass before a car or proper motorbike can be acquired stretches ahead like some hideous vision of eternity. The only acceptable escape from the drudgery of the bus and bicycle was the sports moped. Honda and Suzuki were at it, plus Garelli and even, I think, Moto Guzzi.

But the Fizzie was the one. Occasionally purple but usually yellow, its name in the teenage vernacular was derived from the phonetic implication of the legend on its side panel and invoked perfectly the character of the thing, even if it was a poor onomatopoeia for the exhaust note, which was more like rin-bin-bin. Owning the Yamaha was the ultimate and all-consuming desire of every right-minded coeval of mine. My mate Simon reported in some detail on a pioneering carnal encounter with a girl called Julie in a quiet bus shelter, but no one was impressed by that. Fischer's dad had bought him a Fizzie.

Obviously, I never had one. I honestly think my mother would have preferred to see me playing with a used hypodermic than riding what was, when all was said and done, a motorbike. Even the ultimate authorities eventually realised the folly of allowing 16-year-olds to own these things, and in 1978 the legislation was changed to restrict them to a top speed of 30mph. Ironically, the requirement for pedals was dropped.

Today, almost thirty years later, and since my mum wasn't looking, I finally rode a Fizzie. On the downside, it will only really do about 45mph, and not the 60 widely claimed. But here's what truly amazed me. It harks from the era of watch straps wider than the watch itself, of nylon paddock jackets, Barclay James Harvest albums, high heels for men, Old Spice and Liebfraumilch, all of which is the landfill of an earlier life. But not the FS1-E.

In fact, it is the first exception I have encountered to my own self-imposed rule that says you should never meet your heroes or revisit an old desire. I already know that the Lamborghini Countach was better as a poster than as an actual car. It's possible that Brian Cant and Derek Griffiths are just a pair of old bores. *Starsky & Hutch* is not half as good as it seemed at the time, the Muppets aren't actually funny and the same Julie who reduced my mate to ruins in the bus shelter is now probably a mother of three with a subscription to *Heat* magazine. The Fizzie, though, with just 49cc and 4.8bhp, turns out to be as exhilarating as I always imagined it must be.

And, in case anyone out there can help, I still want one really badly.

Out of date and out of mind

As far as I can tell, absolutely everyone in motoring journalism, the *Top Gear* production office, the motor trade, internet car chatrooms and down on the street is raving about the new Fiat Panda 100hp.

If you haven't seen it yet, it's a bit like a normal Fiat Panda only with a 1.4-litre engine, fatter wheels and a bit of light bodykit. I, and I alone, think it's pointless. I haven't actually driven it but I'm absolutely certain it's a waste of money.

To understand my dissent we need to take a look at the television; more specifically, at my television. Whenever I become embroiled in one of those lengthy discussions about consumer electronics I tell everyone that I, too, have one of those fatscreen TVs, and hope they're not really listening. Once the boasting starts I announce, calm as you like, that it's a 32-inch model, but without letting on that I'm referring to its depth.

Thing is, I bought a new television recently – by which I mean within the last ten years – and, subconsciously, I think that's it. I have my television set, and I can relax in the knowledge that I will never have to go through the appalling inconvenience of going out to buy another one. I also bought a radio for the home once. It was so long ago that pretty much every part of it except the valves is made of wood.

That was long before I bought the computer on which I'm writing this column but, to be honest, that wasn't in this century either. I hear that the 'podcast' is becoming a popular medium for the dissemination of news and opinion; even Mazda cars does them now, and there is currently one on the web from its UK marketing director in which he discusses the hot hatch sector. Unfortunately, expecting an iPod to connect with this machine is a bit like expecting Alexander Graham Bell's telephone to take pictures. In any case, most web pages come out as Egyptian these days.

I could go on. I shall. A while back the brushes on the electric motor of my washing machine wore out, so I summoned Hotpoint service. The earnest young man who arrived at my house – an obvious aficionado of domestic labour-saving devices – was utterly dumbstruck at what he saw. He was like an AA man who had been called out to a routine home start and discovered that someone was still using Tim Birkin's blower Bentley as day-to-day transport. 'Good grief,' he said. 'You must have had this since the 80s.' I didn't like to tell him I'd inherited it in the late 70s.

Back to the Panda 100hp. Regular readers may remember that I bought a Fiat Panda recently, the 1.2-litre version with 65 hp. I paid for and collected it almost exactly 24 hours before the new 100hp model was announced. And I admit I was a bit annoyed. It was a bit like buying a replacement round-pin plug for the kettle and coming home to find a man fitting the new square-pin socket to the kitchen wall.

And yes, I suppose I am the bloke who would have bought the Betamax video player, the Super 8 camera, the Sta-prest trousers and the Audi 80 with the radical Procon 10 safety system, the one thing that would stop me hitting my face on the steering wheel in the event of an accident.

Or it could be that I'm a bit tight, and that some vestige of a Presbyterian ethic leaves me reluctant to replace outdated possessions that, when all's said and done, still serve me perfectly well, even if they don't feature surround sound, MP3 compatibility, a built-in water purifier, digital reception, Wi-Fi, energy-saving bulbs or indeed 100 hp. The relationship I have with my personal appliances appears to be the one an 85-year-old has with a Honda Accord. Make do and mend, if it ain't broke don't fix it, it'll see me out, etc etc etc.

But there's another way of looking at this. Is there any reason why I should be tormented by the extra 35 horses Fiat is dangling in front of me? Should it worry me more than that my fridge isn't chilling my milk in a totally contemporary way? For a brief moment my 65hp Panda shone brightly as the latest thing. But now there's a superior model, it can simply function as my biffabout city car for decades of escalating obsolescence, just as my record deck does. This has improved it immensely.

There is a lesson for life here, one that right-minded people have known for centuries: choose once, and choose well.

Even if you choose badly.

Rubbish in, rubbish out

I think it was Trevor Baylis, the clockwork radio bloke, who said in a lecture a year or two back that Britain had become 'a nation of shopaholics who had lost sight of the value of production.' And it struck me that he could be right, so I immediately set about becoming an inventor as well.

My track record on this is not good. After almost ten years, I have finally given up trying to persuade the high-street banks to install cash machines with a 'gamble' function. Seems like a brilliant idea to me. Why worry about building supercasinos when normal people can throw away hundreds of pounds en route to the shops? You enter your PIN, ask for, say, £100, and then you have the option to gamble it. You end up with either £200 or sod all, but your account is still debited by the original amount.

But no one likes this, or my theoretical design for a domestic machine that recycles old copies of *Telegraph* Motoring into lavatory paper, thus cutting out Andrex, its delivery infrastructure and the annoying puppy, and thereby allowing you to cut your CO_2 emissions while reading about cars on the khazi. So I've moved on.

My latest thinking concerns shaving. If you're like me – and I know a lot of men are – you will cover your face evenly with foam and then shave it off in such a way that you can see what you might look like with a Hitler tache or Emerson Fittipaldi's bugger-grips. But the effect is always slightly unconvincing.

So what's needed is a range of coloured shaving foams – black, several shades of brown, blond, grey and of course not forgetting older people who were born before being ginger was eradicated. Carrot-tops always look good with beards, and they will see just how like a wizard from a Harry Potter film they could look by using May's 'I can't believe it's not stubble' shave stick.

I've written to Gillette and have so far received no reply. Their objection, I suspect, is that encouraging beard growth has a direct impact on razor sales. They needn't worry. No man in his right mind actually *wants* a beard; we just want a laugh pretending to have one for a few minutes before breakfast. It's merely a novelty item, a passing *divertissement*, like Tiptronic gearboxes. But no.

So I've now applied my mind to motoring. First, and taking my inspiration from celebrity chefs' ranges of cookware and celebrity gardeners' branded trowels, I wrote to Shell suggesting that they market Jeremy Clarkson Unleaded. This would be exactly the same as normal unleaded but dispensed through a pump bearing an image of the great man's face and the legend 'poweeeeer' in big letters. It would make absolutely no difference whatsoever to the performance of your car but would cost 1p per litre more, in return for the warm glow of satisfaction you'd get from the implied advocacy of this towering colossus of tyre destruction.

Why not? As far as I can make out, the Nigella Lawson casserole dish is exactly the same as any other, and won't prevent my own casserole from turning out like anything other than hardcore. It's also ruddy expensive and yet the last time I went to John Lewis, it had sold out.

Here's a better one. Not really an invention at all, just an idea; and not really an original one at that, since Volvo tried it once but seems to have given up on it. I want someone at the British Standards Institute to establish a regulation-sized centre-console car bin and a regulation bin-bag to go in it.

I'm amazed this has never happened. My modest little house is full of bins. There are two bins in the kitchen, a bin in my office, bins in the garage, a bin in the yard for plant clippings, a bin in the bathroom and even a bin in the spare bedroom, so that when my mates stay over after dinner they have something to be sick in. There is a bag to suit each of these bins.

But there is no culture of in-car bins and bags, which is odd when you think of the steady ingress of rubbish headed the way of the typical runabout: American Hard Gum packets, parking tickets, scribbled directions, the leaflet a breakdown organisation gave you at the motorway services, tissues, the groaning partwork that passes for a VAT petrol receipt these days. Tons of the stuff. When I cleaned out my old Range Rover prior to selling it, I found one shoe and a small item of broken garden furniture.

Bins are what separate us from the beasts. You have them everywhere else, you should have one in the car. Apart from anything else, if you own a Mercedes S-class you'll finally have somewhere to put the owner's handbook.

A postcard from France, part III

Dear readers,

There's something that has bothered me ever since I arrived in France and started hanging around with Oz 'I'm getting raspberries' Clarke. And it's this.

In pretty much every arena of human activity, we unashamedly embrace science and its exploitation through industry. Even those who purport to be living on the set of *The Good Life* will marvel at how a DVD player can be bought for as little as £35, or wonder how civilisation ever developed before the mobile phone. Things that were once the fancies of sci-fi writers have become disposable trinkets, and all through the economics and efficacy of manufacturing science and mass production.

And this is a good thing. The world, I'm convinced, and despite what old people tell me, is always getting better. We have more aid to our labours, better means of communicating with our loved ones, less chance of catching beri-beri and more chance of being cured if we do. And all thanks to what an Italian fridge-maker used to call the appliance of science.

And yet . . . when it comes to food and drink, we feel better if it's produced by bucolic peasants in smocks toiling in fields like an illustration from John Duc de Berry's book of hours. We think that to industrialise it is to spoil it, when clearly we believe the opposite of everything else. Why?

This week on my wine tour, for example, I was expected to stand barefoot in a wooden tub of Chardonnay grapes in order to crush them. This, I pointed out to the vintner, was a job that should be done by a machine, and ideally one made by Toyota. But no. The human foot, I was assured, is the best instrument yet devised for gently breaking the skins of the grapes and beginning the process of extracting the juice. What's more, it is the direct involvement of the rustic wine-maker – even if in this case it was me – that assures the character of the finished produce.

There's a lot of this sort of thing on our trip. The harvesting and selection of grapes by hand, the ploughing off a vineyard with a mule instead of a tractor, and some mystical nonsense about earth energy in the nurture of some Merlot crop. All of this gives wine a local flavour, apparently.

But what French wine doesn't offer, it seems, is any sort of consistency, and consistency is the key to modern consumerism. Henry Ford reduced costs by mass production, but before that Cadillac demonstrated that it was the inter-changeability of parts that made it possible. This, in any case, had already been demonstrated in the clockmaking and gunsmithing businesses. Even modern Japanese car factories, which produce cars in 'work cells' and have overthrown many of the old ideas of series production, owe their success to the utter fidelity of the parts they use. It is the art of manufacturing that ensures that a new brake calliper bought from a Ford spares operation will absolutely and unequivo-cally fit your Ford Focus.

Car industry bosses, at least on the quiet, would also admit that the exclusive hand-built car (of which there are very few true examples left anyway) is not really as depend-able as the mass-produced one. It may be rarer and trimmed with more exquisite materials, but it won't actually be as good. All other things being equal, manufacturing is superior to the craft tradition. So why isn't Renault making the wine?

Now I know why. The fact has been widely recorded and trumpeted by the wine fraternity, but the terrain and climate of a country like France really can change significantly within the span of half a mile. A slight increase in altitude, a shift in the composition of the soil, a subtly different geographical relationship to the path of the setting sun: these things really do make a difference. The earth is anything but consistent, so how can its produce be? Maybe the wine bores have a point.

But hang on. The earth may be cussed in Europe, but elsewhere in the world it is utterly uniform. In Australia, New Zealand, Chile and California, for example. There, the terrain is the same for miles on end, the sunshine and rainfall utterly predictable, and the wine business unencumbered by the bloody-mindedness of *Appellation Côntrolée*. And in these places wine is truly manufactured, and almost always to a higher standard than a humdrum French co-operative can manage at the same price.

So in the modern world, you're almost certainly better off drinking Chilean Cabernet and driving a Honda. But misty-eyed romantics needn't despair. The exclusive and very tasty 1988 Chateau Pichon Baron will be available for some time yet.

And I suppose you could always drive a Bristol.

The pointy end of motorcycle purchasing

In one sense, the British public has a moral obligation to pursue the sport of darts. The days when we were compelled to practise archery on the village green, so that we might be prepared to see off invaders, are long gone; yet darts, generally thought to have derived from all that bow-and-arrow stuff, is a convenient way of keeping the eye in, and with the Channel Tunnel the risk of an assault from France is, if anything, worse.

These days, though, the dartboard is generally used to settle debts or establish whose round it is. People have played the stock market with darts and I've seen debates over holiday destinations resolved with a bit of left-hand-nearest-the-bull malarkey. But what about a new motorcycle?

It all began with an everyday pub debate over etymology. What is the difference between a treble and a triple? Treble, we decided, and after several of them, means three times something, as in 'treble 20', i.e. sixty. Triple means three of, as in the three-cylinder Triumph Speed Triple. You can probably guess where this is going.

I've fancied a Speed Triple for a while. I've even managed to save up for one. But because I am wracked by Protestant self-loathing whenever I spend a large sum of money, I cannot bring it upon myself to simply buy a motorcycle. Especially as, when all's said and done, I already have one.

These things have to be earned, and it was decreed that I could have the Trumpet when I'd scored three treble 20s in one go. What's more, the triple treble top (see?) must be achieved during a regular game in which I might at times be obliged to aim for other numbers in order to maintain dignity in the face of my usual opponent, Tony.

Now he's a man who knows his arrows and likes a wee dram afore he throws. One day, when he has achieved true greatness, I shall be in a position to write his biography, a stirring tale of personal triumph over the debilitating effects of leglessness – *Reach for the Scotch*.

My personal darts peak arrives after about three pints, when suppleness returns to the wrist. So after an hour or so during which I was regularly rewarded with the evocative thud of mild steel penetrating the Edwardian oak panelling of the Cross Keys, I had settled into an impressive rhythm of scoring quite well.

In fact, I threw two treble 20s and the pub, had there been anyone else there, would have descended into an electrified silence as, for my third throw, I positioned my right toe against the ancient brass strip burnished and patinated by a million cheating feet. Legs braced, elbow tucked well in, eyes focused, muscles instructed to repeat the impulse that had launched the previous two darts, I released the flashing javelin of salvation.

In the pantheon of blunt things there are old Stanley-knife blades, neglected carving knives and rusty chisels. There is that tool that allegedly makes extra holes in belts and there was the school bandsaw. But the world does not admit of a point more dull than the tip of a dart kept in a jar behind the bar of a local pub. For complex geometric reasons such a dart is more likely to bounce off the thin wire that cruelly divides motorcycling satisfaction from despair, and so it did.

Now the rules (or at least the rules in my pub, and if you don't like them you can go elsewhere) state that if the point of the rebounding dart lands behind the oche, the throw may be taken again. And it might have done. Or it might not. It was difficult to tell, because it had gone behind the radiator.

It says something about the reputation of the place that the sight of two grown men lying facedown on the floor elicited not so much as a murmur from two regulars who chose that moment to enter through the normally hazardous side door next to the board. But once the gravity of the situation had been outlined to them, they, too, dropped without demur to the dusty boards and unanimously declared that I had earned a re-throw.

And so, having brushed the 100-year-old dead spiders from its mangled flights, I launched the dart of joy anew. I cannot deny that the onus was on me to check that the shaft was still firmly screwed to the body of the missile, and that it was because it wasn't that the two separated in flight and the point removed a huge wooden divot from the scoreboard while the tailpiece fluttered pathetically to earth.

As a famous darts commentator once said, there's only one word for that. And neither of them is 'magic'.

The case for cat-nav

Every now and then a piece of technology arrives to provide the long-awaited answer to a question that has troubled man ever since he descended from the trees. The radio telescope, for example, which helped to establish how old the universe is, and how big.

More recently, I believe some of the advances in driver navigational aids may now be in a position to resolve one of the great mysteries of the human condition, a conundrum that has baffled people for hundreds of generations and which has been vexing me this week in particular – namely, where the bloody hell is my cat?

Normally, I don't even want to know where Fusker is. I know that he is, like most cats, something of a community animal. I believe, in fact, that in some countries this fundamental characteristic of cats is recognised to the extent that is not legally possible to 'own' one.

He is a free spirit, a neighbourhood cavorter with the stature of a small loaf and the heart of a lion, hairy-hearted confirmation that, as I've always suspected, the animals are not really our friends. I know he's in and out of everyone's houses, and that he convenes with his cat chums on a garage roof in the afternoon to exchange notes on armchairs, radiators and who's roasting a chicken. For me, it's always been enough that, as night falls, he announces with the clunk of his catflap that it is to my home that he returns to fulfil his role, correctly identified by Woman, as a furry reminder of human neediness.

But now someone else is feeding him, and presumably with wild Scottish smoked salmon, because last night a portion of his favourite free-range Spam was left untouched in the cat bowl. He even turned his nose up at the meaty treats from Sainsbury's, and they seem to think he can taste the difference.

It's a problem because it's time for his tri-monthly worming medicine, which comes in tablet form and is crumbled into his dinner. This stuff is not found in the leftovers from my posh neighbours' Japanese puffer-fish takeaway. As he's not eating his proper food he's not getting his dosage and that's bad for him.

So I need to know where he's going, and there are a couple of ways of doing this. The other day, I met a former MI5 bloke who schooled me in the arts of video bugging. Tiny cameras, about the size of a lentil and connected to recorders not much bigger than a box of Swan Vestas, can be hidden almost anywhere – in a book, in a pot plant, in a wall clock. Amazingly, this stuff is available on the high street. He even had a video camera in the knot of a tie he'd bought from Spy Rack.

But while I could hide the camera in Fuzza's fur, I'd have difficulty disguising the recorder. I think he'd arouse suspicion wearing a rucksack. Then people would know they were being watched and wouldn't behave normally, in the same way that they're not honest when filling in the *Cosmopolitan* sex survey. Also, and like George Formby when he was cleaning windows, I might see something I'd rather not know about.

No: the answer, I believe, lies in the workings of my portable NavMan satnav device, which fits comfortably in the palm of my hand. But it's only that big because it has to incorporate the screen and the little speaker through which the digital harridan berates me. I'm betting that the electronic circuits that deal with the business of decoding the satellites' signals are minute, and would probably fit inside a cat collar.

Meanwhile, my desktop computer has something called a

Wi-Fi device that means it can communicate wirelessly with the box that connects me to the World Wide Web of Lies. The range of this thing must be about the same as the extent of Fusker's territory, since it seems to work in the pub sometimes.

So, incorporate the transmitter in the cat, and I'll be able to watch his movements on a moving map on my screen. Voilà – Cat Nav. Old dears worried about the whereabouts of Fluffy have wanted something like this since the Egyptians turned the cat into a deity. Get on to it, NavMan. There are millions of cats in Britain and no one knows where any of them are. You'll clean up.

And talking of cleaning up: if you're the one feeding my cat and you're reading this, then I hope he pukes right in the middle of your new sitting-room carpet on the day you have it laid. Like he did on mine.

Driving is easy, and that's just as well

For a while now, I've been wondering if cars would be more engaging if they were a lot harder to drive.

Of course, some people like to pretend that driving is a very specialised skill. The Institute of Advanced Motorists, for example, who sometimes seem to imagine that the rest of us have not grasped the enormity of the undertaking.

Then there are track-day driving instructors, who often sound like human resources executives, talking about personal development and building progressively on a skills base. I worry that even our own Stig would sound like this if he could talk, but since he's the result of an early experiment in bionics – his urine is just a stream of transistors – he can't, fortunately.

It would be nice to drive a car knowing that few other people were qualified to do so, but, as I have observed before, it's not like being an Apollo astronaut or a member of Pink Floyd. Everyone I know can do it and I must therefore conclude that it's easy.

By way of illustration, it's interesting to compare a journey in the car with a trip in the little tin 'n' rivets aeroplane I fly. When I walk out of the door to take a spin in the Fiat Panda, I don't even bother to check if the tyres are all inflated. If they're not, I'll know by the end of the road and I can stop and do something about it. But on the aeroplane, the tyre condition is just one of hundreds of things I'm supposed to consider before I even get in the thing. Brake lines as well. It's so complicated that I have to carry a little book reminding me of all the things I'm supposed to look at before I can go anywhere.

They include the hinges on all the control surfaces and the rods and wires linking them all together. I have to check all the lights, the fuel tanks, the fuel itself for moisture or contamination, the condition of the metal skin, the oil level, the brake-fluid level, the prop for nicks and chips, the engine cowlings for security, the functioning of the buzzer that warns of a stall and the heater for the pitot tube. I have to check that the belt driving the alternator is in place, since it's difficult to repair with a pair of tights in flight. I've never done that with a car.

By now it's time to climb aboard, alone, because Richard Hammond will have gone home in a fuming rage of impatience. But don't imagine you can just fire up the engine. You have to check for free movement of the throttle, mixture and carburettor heat levers, for full movement of the controls, that the heating and ventilation works, that all the circuit breakers are in place, that the instruments all work and that the clock is telling the correct time. Now, perhaps, we can put the key in.

But we still can't start the engine. First, it's necessary to turn the electrics on, including the fuel pump, and make sure that the warning lamps designed to indicate failure of some of the above will light up when needed. The engine may have to be primed. Then it's necessary to make sure that no one is standing next to the propeller. Then the starter can be cranked, assuming it's not already dark, in which case it's time to pack up again.

With the engine running, a quick check must be made of oil and fuel pressures, of the vacuum for the instruments, of the output of the alternator, that the twin magnetos that govern the engine's ignition are working properly and independently, and that the radio is on and correctly tuned. And now, finally, and what seems like half a day after I collected the key from the ops room, the aeroplane moves forward.

There are lots of things to check during the taxi to the runway. The brakes, more instruments, the setting for the altimeter, the nosewheel steering, the radio reception. Near the runway, it's necessary to make sure that the engine will run at full power, at idle power, on each set of magnetos, without an unacceptable drop in oil pressure, and without overcoming the brakes. The flaps have to be sorted out, the locks on the door have to be checked, and if Richard Hammond were still there I'd have to tell him how to get out in an emergency.

And now the kite rolls forward and at around 55 knots (slightly more if Hammond is aboard) and the rush of air over the wings, in accordance with the findings of Daniel Bernoulli, rewards us with the gift of flight. But it doesn't get any easier up there.

One instrument indicates the airspeed. But since the air varies, this will be different from the true airspeed. What's more, the aeroplane flies through the air as though it were still, but it might actually be moving across the land. So to go somewhere, I have to know the true airspeed and the wind speed and how this will affect deviation from a true heading calculated from a map but which has to be converted to a magnetic heading in order to use the compass, into which magnetic variation must be factored in order to arrive at a track and real speed across the ground itself. It's said that a good landing is one you walk away from, and a very good landing is one you walk away from leaving a serviceable aeroplane behind. In my view any landing made at the airfield I took off from is a bloody miracle.

And yet ... I like all this stuff. I admit it makes me feel a bit clever, in the way that stockbrokers get a kick out of needing to know the time in New York and Tokyo. Wouldn't mundane car journeys be a lot more involving if there was a lot more to worry about?

To find out, I borrowed a 1922 Buick, to see what driving was like in an era when the motorist was still a minister to a rare and baffling machine, rather than the mere operator of an everyday device. The pedals were the wrong way round, and so were the gears. There was no synchromesh – no roof either, come to think of it – and there were levers on the wooden steering wheel to alter the fuel mixture and the ignition advance for hill climbing and 'fast' cruising. There was some sort of manual fuel pump, no indicators and a cranking handle for starting, which made stalling at the lights annoying for everyone.

And I absolutely hated it. It was far too difficult. After half an hour of driving around at 25mph I was utterly exhausted. This is why old people tend to take driving so seriously. They remember when it was a lifetime's work.

So, to return to my original question: would driving be more interesting if it was a bit more difficult? No. Sorry, I've wasted your time.

That North Pole nonsense

The fundamental problem with any journey to the North Pole is that there are, in fact, two of them: the magnetic North Pole, which is a physical phenomenon, and the true North Pole, which is a cartographical convention established from the shape of the earth and the axis of its rotation. Bored yet? This is only the beginning.

You might wonder why this is. Well, the magnetic North Pole is useful for most basic navigation as it determines the direction of a compass needle. Unfortunately, it moves around a bit over the years, and severely buggers up mapmaking.

Also, for the purposes of dividing the globe into lines of longitude, which relate to time as well as position, the true North Pole is better because it's right at what we think of as the 'top' of the planet. Serious maps are oriented towards true north, and if navigating with a magnetic compass, as most amateur sailors and airmen do, it is important to allow for something called 'magnetic variation'; that is, how many degrees away from true north your magnetic north is. This changes around the planet and is indicated on maps using something called 'isogonal lines'. In London, for example, magnetic variation is currently about 3 degrees west.

Bloody hell.

It's important to establish which North Pole you are talking about when using an expression such as 'let's go to the North Pole'. Technically, if you are at the North Pole, everything is to the south, no matter which way you turn. If you are at the magnetic North Pole, then the true North Pole is to the south, and if you are heading to the magnetic North Pole and find yourself at the true North Pole, the North Pole is still to the north. Unless, that is, you are working to true bearings, in which case you will stand at the true North Pole with your magnetic compass still pointing north, but actually that's south.

Anyway, we decided to head for the magnetic North Pole; or rather, Clarkson and Hammond did. Clarkson, the best off-road driver 'in the world', would go in a Toyota pick-up truck, and Hammond would eschew at least a century of progress and be towed there by some dogs. I didn't actually want to go at all. I hate snow, I hate extreme cold, I hate dressing up and I knew it would involve some camping, since there are no hotels.

But Jeremy insisted, saying I should come along as his navigator. This was pretty insulting really, because navigating to the magnetic North Pole is a simple matter of heading north with a compass, obviously. Even if, starting from Canada, I followed the wrong end of the needle I'd know about it once we got to Mexico.

Now we have completed this great odyssey, I can categorically confirm that going to the North Pole, by whatever means, is a completely futile and miserable exercise. It starts with the special Arctic clothing, all of which is covered in stupid zips that catch in everything and makes a really irritating and deafening rustling noise if you so much as scratch your head. Taking a poo in the Arctic involves removing ten layers of this stuff and then quite literally freezing your nuts off. And that's if you don't get eaten by a bear while your trolleys are down.

You might imagine that an endless vista of snow, interrupted only by the occasional abstract ice sculpture, is something quite beautiful to behold, and it is. For an hour or so. But after a few days it's a bit like looking at a screwed-up sheet of plain A4 paper. Open the freezer compartment of your fridge and look at that for two weeks to get an idea of what it's like.

The extreme cold – minus 30 at times – is a nuisance. Because the atmosphere is extremely dry up there, none of your personal effects ever freezes solid; they just become very cold. However, the instant you spill anything – your gin and tonic, say – then your trousers become part of the landscape. I took a packet of Johnson's baby wipes with me, for the purposes of 'washing', but within ten minutes they'd become a scented iceberg. Only in the Arctic have I been presented with the problem of having to keep my tins of tonic warm enough to drink. And don't imagine that we were nice and warm in the car – we weren't allowed to have the heating on because it would interfere with our special misery-spec Arctic onboard cameras.

I hardly dare remind myself of the camping. It's not just that the tent had to be erected and dismantled every day, or that the zips on that always stuck as well, or even that the rudimentary kerosene stove set light to my face. The real problem was having to share it with Clarkson, who was incapable of helping to put the thing up, even though the job required the use of nothing more than his favourite tool, a hammer.

I'm not a great camper but Clarkson is a worse one. Every night he would zip himself up completely in his cocoon-style sleeping bag, even his head, and then blaspheme into the thick down all night long. It was like sharing a tent with a big sweary maggot.

There was little respite during the day, whatever the day was. Because it was the summer, the sun simply cavorted up and down the sky like some cosmic fairground attraction, and at one point we had a huge row over whether it was lunchtime or midnight. We honestly didn't know. Driving was a simple matter of enduring the constant crashing and rattling of the overloaded Toyota, punctuated by the occasional dull report of another exploding tin of Schweppes as we crept further north (magnetic).

I honestly believe that it was only the drink that kept us going. Even asking Clarkson if he'd like some ice in his G&T

wasn't funny after a day or so. The conversation started well enough, with intelligent debate about politics and geography, but after a few days we were arguing for hours about the significance of just-in-time manufacturing versus the importance of interchangeability of parts, and by day four we had been reduced to food fantasies involving sandwich spread and sausages. I cheered Clarkson up with the caviar and quails' eggs I'd smuggled past the Arctic exploration Nazis, and he rewarded me by shooting my tin of Spam, for which I wish an especially virulent pox upon him still.

And when we finally arrived at the Pole, there was nothing. No monument, no visitors' centre, not even a cairn of ice cubes. It was just more snow. We intended to leave a small *Top Gear* flag we had made, but discovered that we'd forgotten to bring the stick for it.

With the mission accomplished, the doctor we'd taken along as part of our small support team asked me, 'So, James, now you've done it, do you think your life will be better or worse for the experience?'

I decided it would be worse. Because occasionally I would remember it.

A brief history of history

This week, I have been reading a book on the history of the Honda CB750 motorcycle. Very good it is, too. Did you know, for example, that the crankcases of the very early models were cast in sand, and that it was only once production was established that Honda moved over to more efficient die casting? Me neither, until now. Early bikes had painted fork stanchions, whereas later ones were chromed. There's a lot of this sort of thing in *Honda CB750* by Mark Haycock, published by Crowood Press.

I can also recommend *Mercedes SL Series* by Brian Laban (Crowood again). You may not know that much of the oily underpinnings of the original SL, regarded by many as the world's first true supercar, were borrowed from the rather dowdy Mercedes 300 saloon. I did know this, but only because I've read it before.

I like this sort of thing; very detailed analysis of a very particular artefact or event from our past, especially if it's a car, an aeroplane, or something to do with the Second World War. But at the same time, I worry about it. History, I mean. I worried about it at school, too, and all because there seemed to be so much of it.

History, at school, was somehow made interminably dull by a teacher who had some pet theory about enclosure in the Middle Ages and never talked about anything else. But I was dimly aware that there was also some stuff to do with Greeks,

Romans, Egyptians and the Battle of Britain. Later in life I discovered that history is actually fascinating, but at the same time I had to admit that there was even more of it than I first thought. The Aztecs, the Chinese, the Irish potato famine. It just goes on and on for ever, or will if we're not careful.

Civilisation is getting older, and at the same time more and more of our existence is being committed to record. There will come a time when the whole of history is too big to contemplate, and no one person will be able to construct even a sketchy notion of how the world came to be the way it is. Socrates, or Plato, or someone else who was idiotic enough to write things down instead of just keeping it to himself, said that he who will not learn from history is doomed to repeat it. How can we learn from it? It's too big.

This has all been brought home to me over the past few weeks, because I've been working on a BBC series about the history of technology in the twentieth century. Unfortunately, we have only six half-hour programmes in which to address this topic, and it isn't really enough; not when there are already several thousand carefully researched words in a book dealing with one car or motorbike. And the technological achievements of the period 1900–1999 is just one aspect of one century. It doesn't go anywhere near pre-industrial Japanese architecture or the development of Hinduism.

The twentieth century is especially significant to my concerns, because it revealed that the too-much-history menace is a bigger threat than we thought. Not only is history lengthening like a shadow with our forward march through time, it is also, in a sense, expanding backwards with new means of investigation. A lot of what we used to call pre-history – that is, from a time before any records were made – was in fact recorded perfectly well in things like carbon deposits or soil chemistry, which we can now read perfectly well. Now a couple of American physicists have measured the residual radiation from the first fraction of a second after the Big Bang, giving us an echo of the moment of creation itself. So history turns out to be a lot older than we first thought.

My conclusion from all this is that there will eventually have to be some sort of enormous natural catastrophe of the sort Noah experienced, just so the slate can be wiped clean and we can be saved from the tyranny of an incomprehensibly complex past. Double history was already an hour long in 1974. Imagine what it will be like in 4050.

And this brings me back to the car. Doom merchants, environmentalists and cod philosophers say its invention was a disaster, and that it will ruin the world. How can it? Its presence occupies the same time as the twinkling of a star in the true span of history, which, as we have seen, will end soon anyway.

And next time around, there's a good chance that Middle East politics, health and safety or Ralph Nader will be invented first, in which case it will never be allowed anyway.

Bring on the flood.

Give me a car, not a cuddly toy

There are several reasons why I could never feel entirely comfortable driving a G-Wiz, even if I managed to overlook the rule of life that says a gentleman does not drive a plastic car.

Firstly, it's a battery-powered electric job, and I've never been able to drive such a thing without constantly worrying about what will happen if I run out of juice. It's all very well claiming that it does the equivalent of 600 miles per gallon, or arguing that all petrol stations should offer a few three-pin sockets, but the fact remains that it has a range of only forty miles or so and takes at least six hours to recharge. Six hours is a long time, even compared with that brief glimpse of eternity that is the age taken to fill up my old Bentley, and with the best will in the world there isn't six hours' worth of entertainment to be had at the Happy Bean coffee stop.

Because it's electric, it's green. But is it? How do you know where the electricity has come from? Has it come from a wind-mill in George Monbiot's garden, or a power station fuelled with old tractor tyres? The other day Sainsbury's offered to sell me some electricity, and some of their vegetables come from Israel.

But never mind any of that. What would bother me above everything else is that it's a bit cute. Why? Why can't it just look like a car?

I realise that if you're designing a truly small car, some

aspects of legislation, and the simple fact that people don't become smaller while they're driving, would make it difficult to style it on the lines of the Lamborghini Gallardo. The lights have to be a certain height above the road, which means they may have to stick up a bit. There's a limit to how low the roof can be, so a short car will end up being disproportionately tall. But this is no excuse for making the Smart fortwo look like two frogs mating.

Cuteness in small cars is a very disturbing trend. I've heard psychologists talk of something called the 'Bambi Effect', which explains the way nature makes the offspring of all intelligent mammals very attractive, so that their parents will feel more inclined to look after them. This seems to work very well for babies and kittens, but driving around in Bambi is taking it a bit far. It's also rather unmanly.

Some cars that are more oochy-coochy-coo than they perhaps needed to be include the Smart, the Nissan Micra, the Toyota Aygo and its relatives, the Daewoo Matiz and the Ford Ka. Now we have the Mitsubishi iCar. I haven't driven it yet but it would appear to be quite well thought out. But did the headlights really need to be that doey? Does it really need a half-witted smile and those chubby cheeks to work? One suspects not.

To my eye, too much cuteness makes a small car look as though it's apologising for even trying to be one in the first place. Cute small cars make me think of those dull grey-suited executives who wear comedy ties because, hey, they're dead funny really. A cute small car seems to say, look, I know I'm just small and a bit pathetic, but look at my face! How could you not love it?! That would be like kicking a puppy!

Not only can this be rather embarrassing, it also perpetrates the notion that small cars are essentially rubbish. A cute small car is a bit like someone who begins an anecdote by saying 'It was really funny . . .', which means it wasn't. Tommy Cooper never said that, and no one ever imagined that the Rolls-Royce Phantom should be in any way a proper sweetie.

This is where we're going wrong. Not only can small cars be perfectly good as cars per se, they can also be among the most entertaining you can lay hands on, and this much needs to be reaffirmed through the offices of sensible, adult styling. The only excuse that needs to be made for a small car is that you have one because you enjoy driving too much to tolerate a big one.

I say this because I've really fallen for my Panda; for its sense of urgency, its liveliness, the eager thrum of its piddling 1.2-litre engine, and the pure hilarity to be had from chucking it at a small roundabout. It doesn't offer the visceral thrill of the Porsche, but in many ways it serves up more cerebral pleasures, which in themselves attest to a more advanced state of the human condition.

It's a great car, and even better when you consider how easily Fiat could have ruined it. They could have lost their bottle and made it really adorable.

We are not amused

I've decided that I'm jolly glad I'm not the Queen of England. I think it must be really boring.

True, she's probably never had to open a curtain or wash her own smalls, but on the other hand, she can't slip down the Windsor Castle for a swift pint and a game of arrows, and though she may be heir to a throne that once seated the empress of India, she still can't sneak out for a crafty late bhuna with Phil at the drop of a crown.

Being the queen *and* a car enthusiast would be a right royal pain in the arse. When you're the queen, presumably the world's top car makers queue up with lavish gifts of bespoke motors. But you have to find a bloke in a hat to drive them for you, because once out on the road you're at work, and expected to sit in the back and wave at the plebs. The Rolls-Royce Phantom series, for example, is one of the world's most expensive and exclusive ranges of cars. The queen has owned a whole string of them but I doubt she has driven one, ever. Even I've driven a Phantom.

I know Aitch Em agrees with me on this one, because for many years she kept a Rover P5 saloon in the Palace mews purely for recreational driving. A while back, I rang up and asked if I could have a go. This, I thought, could go one of two ways. I could end up in the Tower with no head, or our sovereign might see fit to reward me for my loyalty with some small token of her appreciation. Cornwall, perhaps. After some harrumphing and long telephonic pauses while people walked very slowly up and down long corridors, the keeper of ye queen's key fob agreed to lend me the old girl for an hour. The Rover, I mean.

'Bloody hell,' I thought, as I selected drive and trundled away, 'I'm driving the Queen's car'. 'That's a nice old Rover,' said an elderly bloke through the open window. 'I'm afraid it's not actually mine,' I replied. 'It's the Queen's.' He began to back away with an alarmed expression like people do when confronted by a dangerous drunk. But it really was the Queen's car, not a trapping of state occasion. Somewhere (though not, sadly, in the glovebox, or I'd have nicked it) is a V5 registration document proclaiming the 1972 P5 to be a one-owner vehicle and the property of Elizabeth Windsor, a lady.

As one constantly torn between unswerving loyalty to the crown and outright support for a republic, I found my monarchic motoring experience quite persuasive. The editor of *Country Life* once proclaimed the Queen to be 'cool', and I think he's right. The P5 is a cool car to have if you could have any car in the world. David Beckham has a brand new Bentley, but he's only the king of football. The Queen's the Queen and has one of these, so I want one, too.

There's something very comforting about the royal Rover. It's original, unmolested, patinated with age and use and, I'd like to say, it smells faintly of the Royal We, but as that isn't actually true, and as relations between the media and the Palace are strained, I'd better not. I'm hoping that by now there is a little brass plaque on its dashboard, like the ones seen on those old Le Mans Bentleys, to proclaim that this particular P5 was driven by Her Majesty Queen Elizabeth II of England and her humble servant James May, who may be found at the sign of the Cross Keys, Hammersmithe.

But my new-found royalist tendencies took a few knocks on the journey. The first thing I noticed was the fuel gauge. There's more four-star in the tank of my Atco lawnmower, and I haven't lived anywhere with a lawn for fifteen years. You'd have thought that the Queen, of all people, would have been able to afford to put in a tenner's worth down at Tesco.

I also couldn't help noticing that there wasn't a valid tax disc. There wasn't an expired one, either; in fact, there wasn't even a tax disc holder. So I have to pay road tax to use the Queen's highway, but the Queen herself doesn't? I suppose she thinks she owns the road. As usual, there's one law for the Queen and another one for the rest of us.

Most disappointing, though, was this. In my own car, I keep a tin of those boiled travel sweets. On the lid is a little crest and the words 'By appointment to Her Majesty the Queen.' I've always understood this to mean that these are the sweets the Queen herself eats on the long haul up to Balmoral. That, in fact, is why I buy them.

But in the centre console of the Queen's car? Nothing.

A load of horse's arse

Regular readers will know of my uneasy relationship with the countryside; with its mud, darkness, terrible smells, unsociable-hours animal noises and strangely-dressed people making their own chutney.

Recently, I've spent quite a bit of time driving through the countryside (since that's what it's for) and there's a lot about it I like very much, especially in Britain. I like the way that, over the course of a mile or two, the widescreen vista can shift from wild rolling hill to swaying cornfield to stone-walled patchwork to verdant hedgerow and then to wooded glade, where a member of the public walking his dog is about to discover a body.

But there's a lot that has been baffling me for years, notably some of the signs. Now quite often you will see one at the end of a driveway saying something like FREE RAGNE EGG'S £2 1/2 DOZ, and I can see why that might draw the odd inner-city escapee in. No matter how fresh the eggs in your local supermarket, they will never offer quite the same fleeting fluffi-ness as those popped in the boiling pan while still warm from the cow.

The other day, though, I came across a piece of cardboard propped against the gate at the end of an enormously long driveway on which had been writ large, in crayon, POTATOES. At first I thought this was another invitation to buy, but how could it be? I don't believe anyone has ever driven through the countryside and been seized by a sudden craving for a potato. Potatoes are not a time-sensitive foodstuff. I can buy them from the newsagents where I live, they last for months in the bottom of the fridge and may even reproduce if I'm lucky. So what was this sign? A celebration of the fecundity of Arcadia? A boast? Or what?

What it really meant, I decided, was something like 'Potatoes. See? You come out here in your shoes and your fancy car, but you hadn't thought about potatoes, had you? And where did you think they came from, eh? Not from your feeble urban garden paved over to facilitate off-street parking, that's for sure. And don't you forget it'. It was a riposte, really; a way for our ever more-beleaguered bucolics to remind us townies that just because we're free to drive around the countryside, that doesn't mean we will ever truly 'understand' it. I also saw a sign that said MANURE. Same sort of thing. The obverse would be me erecting a sign outside my house saying ELECTRICITY or SEWERS.

I like this theory and I'm sticking with it, because it finally explains why horseboxes and horse lorries always have the legend HORSES painted across their tailgates. Every time I come up behind one I wonder what, exactly, my reaction should be to the news that there are horses in the vehicle in front, other than amazement that anyone should still be using such things. Why do I need to know?

People who display those tiresome 'Baby on Board' stickers can always argue – with some conviction, I suppose – that they are there to remind the emergency services, in the event of a sudden flood or multistorey car-park collapse, to rescue the infant that might otherwise go unnoticed on the back seat. But this is never going to be an issue with a horse, especially as any approach to a horsebox ultimately rewards you with a view of the beast's arse. So I wonder if this is just another example of the country folk trying to put us in our place.

Still, let's try being a bit more sympathetic here. There is a country code for drivers just as there is for walkers, and it may be worth reminding ourselves what it is. We should slow down for the village, so as not to alarm anyone deep in a reverie of walnut-pickling or corn-dolly manufacture. We should give a wide berth to cyclists and ramblers. We should not park in gateways or narrow lanes where we might impede the movements of tractors, and when encountering a horse actually being ridden on the road it is important to drop down a couple of cogs and get by as quickly as possible, thus minimising the animal's discomfiture.

And if you do find yourself behind a large vehicle transporting horses by road, there are some things you should definitely not do. Most importantly, never let a horse know that you are afraid. Do not discharge a handgun out of the driver's window, and never, ever dress up in the brightly-coloured dragon costume from a Chinese New Year celebration and dance around in the road.

Not that any of you were going to.

Porsche – taste the difference

Here's the scene. I'm in my Porsche, I've been driving through suburbia for some time, and I'm slightly bored. But then, as the houses peter out, I finally spot a good-looking stretch of derestricted A-road, and I think to myself, 'Wahey. This looks good. I think I'll put it in sport mode.' I press the button, the legend 'sport' appears on the little display in the rev counter, and off I jolly well go.

I should point out that this is the first car I have ever owned with a sport button, and I've been utterly delighted by it; by the thrill of being able to reconfigure my car to suit the driving environment, or whatever it would say in the owner's handbook if I could be bothered to read it. But all of a sudden, I'm beginning to feel like a bit of a mug. After ten months, I've had to acknowledge that the sport button in the Porsche Boxster doesn't really do anything at all.

Now before all the Porsche bores write in, I do know that in sport mode the parameters of the traction control are relaxed so that the skilled driver can display his prowess by gathering up a whiff of incipient oversteer with an armful of opposite lock, or whatever it is men in pubs claim to be doing of a weekend. But nothing is of less interest to me. That's just something that happens in *Autocar* magazine.

But at the same time, the electronic brain that governs all this also sharpens up the throttle response, making the car more lively, more frisky, more responsive to the inputs of the dedicated helmsman. Or does it?

No. I've just done a simple experiment. I drove along a dual carriageway at a constant 60mph, throttle held precisely, and in sport mode. Then I turned sport mode off. The car faltered, and then carried on as normal at about 57mph. As far as I can make out, sport mode simply means slightly less pedal travel is required for the same result.

There's quite a lot of this sort of thing about; of products designed to be as good as possible and then downgraded slightly so that we, the consumers, can either press a button or pay a little extra money to have what we wanted in the first place. In the BMW M6, for example, the driver can twiddle the i-Drive control to select either 400bhp or the full 500bhp. But why, if you'd bought the M6, would you want 400bhp?

The Bentley Continental GT owner can twirl a similar knob to select the 'comfort' setting on the car's suspension. Why isn't it just like that anyway? Under what circumstance would you want a Bentley to be anything other than comfortable?

These things may give you a temporary warm feeling, a sense that car makers are considering their customers and allowing them to tailor a car to their individual requirements, but if you think about it a bit harder you'll soon realise that they are just wasting your time.

Elsewhere, a friend of mine has a vacuum cleaner with a button marked 'Turbo Power'. Press this, and full suction is delivered. But surely it's always required. No one wants to leave some of the dust on the carpet.

Now I think about it, I'm becoming suspicious of Sainsbury's Taste the Difference range. I've always bought Taste the Difference cheddar cheese – it's a little bit more expensive than the other stuff, but it's also a little bit nicer. Now, though, I'm wondering why they don't simply make all the cheese taste that good. I'm worried that they're deliberately producing mediocre cheese so I can go through the motions of selecting the good stuff.

What really bothers me about the sport button is the idea that, as a Porsche owner, I would somehow want to 'buy in' (as the marketing people would put it) to a little bit of extra sportiness. I 'bought in' to the notion of a sports car when I went in to the Porsche showroom and handed over a fat cheque for the Boxster instead of veering off to the Citroën garage and buying a C6.

In any case, we've got this the wrong way round. All of Sainsbury's cheese should be top notch, save for a small selection of leftover 1970s British Rail sandwich cheese, branded as the Taste the Awfulness range, there to remind us how much worse it could be.

And the Boxster should be built as a supreme sports car but fitted with a special button that makes the steering vague, the ride choppy, the handling floppy, the interior plastics too shiny, the engine less powerful but the fuel consumption worse.

This button should be marked 'America'.

A postcard from France, part IV

Dear readers,

By the time you read this, my French wine tour will be over. I will have crossed the silver sea (which serves it in the office of a wall, or, as a moat, defensive to a house etc) and returned to the sceptred isle.

And as I return early on a Saturday, I can already tell you exactly what I'll be doing. If it's between 9 and 11 in the morning, I'll be drinking several large mugs of builders' tea made with the one ingredient that the French, for all their talk of *terroir*, cannot readily provide; that is, fresh milk not ruined by the UHT process. I know it's a bit predictable for me to bang on about the inability of foreigners to knock up a cup of char, but let's not be soft about this. If the people of Somerset can make brie, the people of Lyon should be able to make tea. The town is almost named after a tea-room, after all.

From around 11 to about one in the afternoon, I'll be in the Ritz (not *that* Ritz – it's a cafe at the end of my road), after which I'm going to have a long lie down with my cat, during which I hope to shake off the terrible *'Allo 'Allo* accent I've accidentally acquired. By eight I'll be ready for dinner, which I imagine will be either cod and chips or a chicken tikka bhuna, after which I shall retire to the local pub and shut the lid on my holiday wine romance with several pints of Fullers. That lot should see me pretty much back to normal.

There are quite a few things I'm not going to miss about France. Oz Clarke's endless talk of the woody high notes; garlic, the devil's own vegetable; shops and indeed whole towns that are shut; camping; bread and jam for breakfast; French motorway sandwiches; and *manigance*. This is a new French word I've learned, meaning, I'm told, a combination of hanky-panky, jiggery-pokery and skulduggery. I'm not entirely sure what any of those things are individually and in English, so imagine how obstructive they are when combined in one Frenchman.

At the same time, there's a lot I *will* miss about this country. Some fine wines, to be honest; some magnificent Frenchmen, but especially the mechanic who rebuilt the Jag's exhaust after I tore it off on an old tank trap in the Alsace region. Given the history of the place, it's difficult to know which nation to blame for this. Amusing cheeses, chateaux, lovely D-roads, *babyfoot*, and the sort of ribaldry that can only develop between two blokes on a very long car journey.

And the Renault 4. The Citroën 2CV is perhaps more iconic, and more people would recognise one, but it is the Renault 4 that truly endures. The cardboard Citroën is becoming surprisingly rare these days, but the Renault is still everywhere. You cannot drive for more than an hour in France, and often only for ten minutes, without seeing a Renault 4 doing what it was meant to do, which is usually transporting a pig, or something like that. Spotting Renault 4s will never pall as an en-route *divertissement*.

The Renault 4, I suspect, is subject to *Appellation d'Origine côntrolée*. If it isn't, it certainly should be. The Renault 4, as the president himself once said, speaks volumes for France. It is more than a simple people's car, it is the wheeled totem of France's desire to retain so many of its peasantine traditions, it's rural bedrock. It is not a classic coveted by enthusiasts, as the Renault Dauphine or Citroën Big 6 is. It is merely an old car that refuses to give up.

Italy has a car like this in the original Fiat Cinquecento. They are still around in huge numbers, confirming the efficacy of the original simple design in their ability to keep going. Like the Renault 4 in France, they are not preserved relics. They are simply still current. People are driving Renault 4s and Fiat Cinquecentos because somehow, and in direct contravention of all logic, it still makes sense to.

I do not think that Britain has a car like this. We have the Morris Minor, the MkII Jaguar, the original Mini, and the MG Midget. Very British they certainly all are, but in very different ways. And they are now largely in the hands of devotees. There is not one single and ubiquitous car that feels like the product of some government initiative designed to reaffirm The British Way.

The Renault 4 is like that, a car that rumbles on in open defiance of the new world order, and in bloody-minded denial of everything that has happened since.

A bit like the French wine business, really.

The future of motor racing, and it's cheap

Every now and then, over at *Top Gear* TV, we have something called an 'ideas meeting'. I suppose other people would call it 'the pub', but as far as we're concerned we are confronting the white heat at the very kernel of creativity, and if industrial lager is needed to keep it at bay, so be it.

An ideas meeting involves everyone on the production team and anyone can, and does, contribute something, even me. The other day, I piped up with 'How about some classic motorsport?' Well, it went so quiet I could hear the producer's clothes rotting.

And I sort of understand why, really. In the phrase 'classic motorsport' I struggle to find a single word that would have caused us to break step in the delirious headlong rush to the discussion about the exploding caravan or the Stig-in-a-Zonda scene. And indeed we didn't.

Apart from anything else, motor racing, at any level, involves a lot of things I don't really approve of: dressing up, taking it seriously, being on time, and oversteer, which is nothing more than a leftwing plot. The beauty of the motor car is that it has liberated the common people and allowed them to stray far and wide, so the idea of using it to arrive at the point you started from two tenths of a second sooner than you did last time flies in the face of everything I hold dear about cars. The car is the most poignant instrument of progress the world has produced, so using it to go nowhere seems strangely ironic.

Even so, I can't believe that motor racing is as boring as it often is. Which is why I have come up with the 1275cc challenge. The producer obviously isn't interested and won't let us talk about it, so I'm going to do it here instead, since this is my column and he can't stop me.

It will take the form of a hillclimb – a hill in every country is pretty easy to find – and will be an international series with appropriate television coverage. As with all proper motor racing, there is a strict formula to keep the playing field reasonably level. But this time it does not hamper technical progress or imagination, it simply keeps it all at pocket-money prices. It's a vision of egalitarian motorsport, and first came to me while I was driving along in my Rolls-Royce.

The car must have been powered, when in production, by the 1275cc variant of the venerable A-series engine. It must retain this engine, and it must be road-legal, with an MoT. The two obvious contenders are the 1275 MG Midget and one of the later editions of the original Mini. Sound examples of these are available for £1500 or so and can also be enjoyed on the road when you're waiting, like Steve McQueen, between races. This ensures that the technical advances forged on the track will translate directly to the car you drive on the road, largely because it will be the same one.

Already, this strikes me as interesting. We have a low, light rear-drive car versus a short, upright front-drive one. For decades people have been arguing in pubs about which layout is best, so now we'll find out in the unforgiving arena of cheap competition against the clock. Hammond can be in the Midget, since he already has one, and I'll take the Mini, as I've owned several and still have the Haynes Manual. Providing the car fits in with the simple criteria mentioned above, anything goes.

Now we arrive at the great stumbling block of motor racing. Make the rules of the formula too vague, as I appear to have done here, and somebody very clever will find a way to gain an insuperable advantage with ground effect or traction control or something like that. The rules are then made ever tighter in the interests of maintaining a good viewing spectacle but the outcome is predictability and the stifling of inventive talent. So here's the clever bit.

The second part of the formula, and the only other rule, applies not to the car itself but to the team's toolbox. Only manually-operated hand tools can be used in the preparation and maintenance of the racing car, and electricity and compressed air are banned.

So you can do what you like, but you can only do it by hand. No one can re-bore the engine to 1500cc, because that requires a machine tool, which is not allowed. Similarly, it will be impossible to trim a few thou off the cylinder head to improve the 'squish', unless you're so brilliant you can do that sort of thing with a file. You can fit a turbo or bigger brake calipers, but only because you can do that with one of those all-in-one toolkits from Halfords.

There is even an incentive here to drive intelligently. Pit stops are obviously to be avoided, because without compressed air wheel-changing will become an interminably tiresome task involving wheelbraces and blisters.

You can widen the track and fit fatter wheels if you want, but if the car is to pass an MoT – which, remember, it must – it will then need bigger wheel arches. If you can't do this with a sheet metal bender and a pop rivet gun, you're stuffed. Excellent. This simple tool rule means a cash-strapped teenager in a lock-up is no worse off than a team entered by Williams.

Best of all, because electricity is banned under the formula, there can be no laptops and tiresome telemetry. That sort of thing is boring and more to the point expensive, which penalises the poor people. Here is a form of racing that rewards artisanal skill and resourcefulness rather than the big budget stemming from a corporate sponsorship deal. What could you possibly spend the money on anyway? More spanners and Nomex? It won't help you win.

I can't help thinking this is all rather brilliant. We're always looking for the future of motorsport. We've tried the MPV challenge and half-car racing, but neither of them quite caught on. This, I believe, will. It will be fun to take part in, fun to watch, instructional, educational and, most importantly, cheap as chips.

By my calculations, we could produce a new world champion for a total outlay of around £2000.

Cars are rubbish

Recently, a friend of mine gave me a vintage telephone as a gift. You know the sort of thing – one of those brightly-coloured 70s types, with a comedy receiver and a big dial with finger holes in it, but fitted with modern innards so it can be plugged straight into a normal phone socket.

And, having used it, I now understand why the homes of some of my childhood friends were equipped with telephone tables. Remember those? They had a sort of pouffe arrangement to sit on, a flat surface for the instrument itself, and a drawer for the Yellow Pages.

I thought these people were dead posh. They must have been, if every other requirement of their lives was already so well furnished that they could afford a dedicated piece just for telephoning. But now I realise that the telephone table evolved simply because dialling was so bloody tiring.

Come round and try it if you don't believe me. You have to insert your finger in the hole corresponding to each individual number, haul it around to the little stop, and then wait for it to return to the start ready for the next one. It takes ages. In its favour, the size of your phone bill is automatically limited by the amount of damage your index finger can sustain.

And it's got worse. In 1976 my parents' phone number featured eight digits. Now it has eleven. Doesn't sound like much of a difference, but two of the new ones are noughts, and the nought is right at the beginning of the dial. In the time it takes to whir its way back to first position I can sense my beard growing.

It only takes a few seconds longer to dial with the old phone than it does with the new push-button type, but in this day and age it feels like a month.

Dialling is not the only thing that has speeded up in my lifetime. Data retrieval is another. If, when I was a student, I needed to look up some facts or figures, I had to get up, have a shower, get dressed, put some shoes on, walk to the library, sign in, look up the book I needed in a card index, find it, find the information I wanted, write it down on a piece of paper, walk all the way back to my house and fall into a coma of exhaustion. Now, of course, I can just look up whatever I need on the internet. And yet I become incandescent with impatience if the time taken for the page to render on the screen is much more than the twinkling of an eye.

When I mentally tot up all the time saved in a typical life through the good offices of things that are now much quicker – phones, computers, microwaves, dishwashers, self-service supermarket checkouts, cash machines, drive-through restaurants and so on – I end up wondering why we haven't all become concert pianists in the eternity of leisure time we must have. But we haven't, because we've filled it with other things, and all of them are still, in truth, too slow.

Here we arrive at the real problem of the car. It's not pollution or congestion, or even the cost of the thing. The problem is that cars are creakingly pedestrian by the standards of everything else we do. They're barely faster now than they were when I was a child. Meanwhile, even tin openers are geared for higher speeds now than they were in the 70s. And that's still not fast enough.

Last weekend, for example, I drove to see an old mate who lives in Devon. The journey took three hours. Three hours! Three hours looking out of a window at the arse ends of diesel Vectras and the like. There is no other activity in my life on which I spend such lengthy and uninterrupted stretches of my time.

This is why the car will not be the ruin of the world, as some are claiming. Soon, most people will be sick of it entirely, and all because it's too slow to be of any use. Concorde was retired not because it was too noisy or too wasteful of resources or too expensive; it was because it wasn't fast enough. A journey that took only half as long as it did on a 747 was still a lifetime in an age when you can download a whole album in a minute without even having to put your trousers on. The car will be a victim of its own sloth, just as the horse was.

I believe, in fact, that it will be usurped by something that moves through the largely unexploited medium of the air above our heads, and at truly huge speeds. The trip to Devon will then take just a few minutes, leaving plenty of time for piano practice.

But the car will not disappear entirely, and to understand why not you only have to look at Britain's canals. I doubt that any coal or jute is being moved on them nowadays, because canals, too, eventually became too slow. But canals are being reopened all the time, and they are all full of gaily painted narrowboats crewed by enthusiasts of rustic musical instruments. These people are simply enjoying boating as a hobby.

I'm sure cars will turn into a hobby as well. At the moment it is immoral to price people off the road, because they have no choice in the matter. Most of them would rather not be there anyway. But when the roads are reserved for those who are simply having a laugh, road tax can be raised to £2000 a year to pay for the upkeep. Why not? No one will be forced to drive; they'll be crossing the country at 1000mph in antimatter-powered levitating balls, and then settling down to a few hours of Chopin. In any case, plenty of people spend more than £2000 on golf-club membership or skiing equipment. We can have road pricing, too. When driving is just a game, road pricing will seem no more unreasonable than having to pay to use the pool table in the pub.

Which sort of brings me to the new Porsche 911 Turbo. As a means of getting anywhere quickly, it's just as useless as my Fiat Panda. But imagine how much fun you'll have in a car that powerful when you don't need to be anywhere in particular.

Er, cars are great

I have to admit that I was not initially very enamoured of
the basic Skoda Fabia 1.2 five-door. I honestly preferred the
minicab that had taken me to the airport at the beginning of
the journey, and as the man driving it was the sort of chap who
earned a living getting up at 5a.m. to drive someone like me
around, you can assume that his life had not gone especially
well and that he therefore had a crap car.

But this seemed worse. I was in Andalucia, southern Spain,
for recreational reasons and, as usual, had hired a car at Seville
airport. I always go for the most basic bracket, because I'm a
bit tight and I prefer to spend my holiday pocket money on
tapas and *platos combinados*. And as a regular customer of
vehicle group A I enjoy the delicious moment of doubt when I
wonder if I'll get a Clio (which I like) or a small Peugeot (which
I don't).

Still – it's only a hire car and, as P.J. O'Rourke famously
observed, few things handle with such aplomb. I would add
that there is no other vehicle in the world that inspires less
concern for the longevity of its tyres or the condition of its
valve train.

But here's the first thing that always strikes me. If I borrow
the most basic version of a small hatchback from its manufacturer – for the purpose of road testing, say – it's never as
basic as the one I get at an airport. Maybe a special low-spec
edition is built for hire car companies whose clients, they know,

will always drive it in the spirit Enzo Ferrari intended. Maybe manufacturers always sneak in a few small extras that make what is purportedly the 'entry level model' seem so much nicer than it really is – optional upholstery in a bright colour scheme, some electric windows in the back, a nicer gearknob, perhaps?

Either way, no matter how firm you are with the salesman, regardless of how far you've stretched your meagre car-buying budget, and even if you're one of those people who believes adamantly that a car is just something to take you from A to B, you will struggle to leave a Skoda showroom with a Fabia as boggo as the one I was driving. It looked as though it had fallen off the production line before it had reached the end.

The interior, for example, was finished in the following complementary hues: grey. The carpets were some sort of underlay. The wheel trims were made from the leftover linings of Christmas-biscuit family assortment tins, and the tailgate from the tin itself. The wheel rim was hard and the facia was the single biggest injection moulding in the long history of plastic. I hated it just sitting there.

Then I drove it. Hated it, because it was of course a diesel. Except that at the first refill, when the diesel nozzle wouldn't fit in the filler neck and the symbol of a green pump mocked me from the inside of the flap, I had to acknowledge that it wasn't. This only increased my rage. The steering was definitely too light, the suspension was too bouncy, and all the stations on the radio were in Spanish, although this wasn't necessarily Skoda's fault.

So the first hundred miles or so of the trip, from Seville to the ancient city of Córdoba, was really a protracted and largely unprintable first drive delivered solely for the benefit of Woman, who at the end of it hated me as much as I did the car. At the hotel, I handed the keys and whatever their equivalent of a shilling is to the bellboy and told him I didn't want to see the Skoda again until it was time to go home.

But of course, after a few days of looking at local historic buildings and admiring the trees, it was suggested that a drive through the Sierra Nevada might be nice. I didn't actually think so, but you know how it is, so the Fabia was dragged out and again refilled, with no less astonishment, with unleaded.

Off we went on the main road leading south to Granada, a steady stream of words that don't appear in the Collins English/Spanish Pocket Gem dictionary flowing from the open driver's window like discarded orange peel. I still didn't like it.

Then we turned off onto smaller side roads through typical southern European villages, where men sit in plastic chairs on the pavement all day and signs warn of the Bandos Señoras, the traditional Andalucian Bandit Girls, who run wild on the plains and hold up unwary travellers with ornamental souvenir *espadas*. Finally, and mapless, we entered the mountains themselves.

And now something strange happened. Gradually, imperceptibly, and no matter how I tried to resist it, the Fabia slowly began to endear itself to me. I looked forward to long hills, where I could push the gruff little engine and rejoice in its willing grumble. I threw it gaily into tortuous and badly engineered bends that had probably evolved out of the footpaths trodden by weary Moorish settlers hundreds of years ago. As the day wore on, and we became more lost, the pleasure of simply driving gradually usurped my former dissatisfaction with the car itself.

This happens to me now and then, but probably not often enough; that sudden sense that simply being allowed to have something as amazing as a car is a truly mind-blowing privilege. How can it be that for such a tiny outlay at the Seville airport rent-a-car concourse I can end up as some sort of latter-day caliph presiding over a whole range of mountains and its ancient forts? Who'd have thought it, eh?

And I end up thinking that we might have got the whole car thing wrong; that we have turned them into monuments to possession and lost sight of what we can actually do with them, which is climb aboard outside our front doors and, if we keep going long enough, arrive at the other side of the world.

Yes, the Ferrari F430 Spider would have been more exciting than the Fabia, but the gap between them is a mere fissure compared with the yawning chasm between the Fabia and no car at all.

The car – any sort of car – is still, and despite what its detractors say, one of the greatest adventures open to us. And to the bored man who picked me up from home in his ancient Rover 600, I'm tempted to say sell everything, chuck in the minicabbing job, and go for a proper drive.

Brochure rage, part I

A few weeks back, I decided it was time to replace the ancient radio and CD player that stands on a shelf in my kitchen, and which, as you can imagine, is my constant companion during the long hours of parmesan-shaving and mixed-leaf-tossing.

The CD player had developed a digital stutter, which could turn even a recording of Bach's St Matthew Passion into gangsta rap, and in a fit of unfed pique, Fusker, the world's most ill-mannered cat, had headbutted one of the little speakers onto the floor, shattering its delicate innards and rendering the output something less than true stereo.

Anyway, I've always fancied one of those Bang & Olufsen radio and multi-CD jobs, the one in which five discs are loaded in a strip and automatically slot themselves into place; a true digital successor to the electro-mechanical marvel that was the Seeburg jukebox. I know hi-fi buffs dismiss this sort of thing as a fashion accessory rather than a true music system, but they're still lamenting the passing of the valve. So I went out and picked up a brochure.

Nice. Very funky cylindrical blue speakers oddly redolent in the shape of the BMW Munich headquarters building. Soft, blinking red lights, remote control and opportunities for wall-mounting in a number of orientations. On such a system, I'd enjoy watching the collected Scott Joplin slide into position almost as much as I'd enjoy listening to it.

But something was wrong. The text didn't seem to talk that

much about sound and function, instead concentrating on a florid explanation of how stylish the B&O was, and what it said about me. There was an image of a man in something approaching a black poloneck – one of those freewheeling and loft-dwelling guru types, I fear – and then there was a gratuitous picture of an Audi A8. There was no reason for it to be there that I could see. It was just an A8 that had been parked in the wrong leaflet.

Now I admire Audis, but I find them a bit pretentious. It's that whole drive-an-Audi-and-be-in-touch-with-the-contemporary-design-zeitgeist thing. And that, I think, was why it was in the B&O brochure; because the sort of person who buys a B&O radiogram is the sort of person who would feel good about driving an Audi. That is, a bit of a square.

So I binned the B&O booklet and bought a radio/CD player made by Roberts who, according to the box, also make radios for the Queen, who is the sort of woman who stores her cornflakes in a Tupperware tub and therefore must be OK. The Roberts is great, comes with a prosaic instruction book, and is exactly the sort of radio for a man who only wanted a radio.

This is not the first time an excess of lifestyle imagery has turned me away from a product that I might otherwise have liked. Years ago, when I bought my house, there were some new riverside apartments being built nearby. So I went to have a look.

Like a Spanish hotel, they weren't yet finished, but that was OK because I knew the wooden hoarding around the site would be liberally adorned with pictures to tempt the prospective buyer into the forthcoming show apartment. And there they were.

Not one of them showed me what I wanted to see, such as the floor plan, the prices, the view from the upper floors, or whether or not the khazi had a window. Instead there were images of people with perfect cheekbones talking on mobile telephones, or looking at laptops in absurd places, or returning from the shops having just spent a fortune on designer spectacles and haircuts. It was all about as much use as a chocolate Maserati.

And almost certainly fatuous nonsense, of course. But what if it were true? I couldn't possibly buy one of these flats in case I ended up living among people who had just moved out of a brochure, and who might keep me awake all night with the racket from their B&O stereos.

Good, solid product information is in danger of being totally usurped by subliminal images that seem designed to remind me that I'm not a male model or successful and high-flying executive. It comes with every consumer product on the shelf. I can't even buy an apple from Sainsbury's without being assaulted by a huge poster showing some grinning idiot whose life and teeth seem to have been immeasurably enhanced by eating one.

Can't buy a car, either. This week, I've been looking at the new Aston Martin V8 Vantage Roadster. Again, I liked the look of it and so, as a fantasist, picked up a brochure.

God in heaven it made me cross.

To be continued . . .

Old bag dies after 25 years as my friend

At the base of the great pyramid of possession is my house, with all that a man may want therein and, as age advances, more. A spice rack (a present, that), books unopened for years, shoes, slightly too much furniture for the space, that Anglepoise lamp with the limp mechanism that I'll mend one day.

Not all of it strictly necessary, I know, because if I go away on a long trip I can condense the essence of my existence into the two Globetrotters that sit on top of the wardrobe, plus a carry-on bag for so-called 'valuables'. The things that make it to the cases must be those that I really need. Or are they?

It follows that what really matters in life is only that which will fit into my Adidas motorcycling backpack. It's no holdall, this, because it won't all go in. It is the bag of truth, to luggage what a rifle is to an American Marine. This is my Adidas backpack. There are many like it, but this one is mine. And I've had it for as long as I can remember; since long before I ever rode a motorcycle. So long, in fact, that it has completed two revolutions of the wheel of fashion, and local youths the age I was when I bought it, and who were then as yet unborn, have pronounced it 'cool'.

It's a simple backpack from an earlier age. It has just two compartments: the main one, for pants, socks, a T-shirt or two and the soft shoes that go on when the biking boots come off, and a small one, for the wallet, the passport, and those other things that lesser travellers might put in something called a 'bum bag'. Once, it was stuffed with trainers and sweatshirts and was heaved with a sigh over the shoulder of a reluctant teenage sportsman. But then it became the bag I took on the bike.

And though the bikes have come and gone, the bag has endured. I have rarely been on a bike without my old backpack. It has crossed the continent with me on something big, its weight on my back a measure of my true worth and a reassuring reminder that the demon of acquisition has been renounced, if only temporarily. To the amateur motorcyclist on a long trip, a small backpack is as liberating as the machine itself.

But it might just as easily have served as a shopping basket, and I have fed six people with the volume of groceries Mr Dazzler deemed I should be able to transport on the humble Honda 90. There has always been a piece of onion skin and some earth in the bottom of the backpack, there to confirm that it is a microcosm of home that I carry behind me, snail-like.

But now it's broken. The end, inevitably, was ignominious. I stuffed one more thing into it, pulled on the zip and it was rent asunder like the curtains in the Temple. In that moment I was suffused with the deep melancholy that comes when some physical link with an earlier existence crumples before you, instantly consigning half a lifetime to memory alone. When the bag burst, a past that I had managed to drag behind me suddenly began to recede.

I have taken the loss of my Adidas backpack very badly, as you can probably tell. Of course I would, because the bond that exists between a man and his bag is a precious thing understood by many – explorers, soldiers, flying doctors, steeplejacks. But it has never been expressed better than it was by Ernest K. Gann in *Fate is the Hunter*, an autobiographical account of his life as an airline and air transport pilot. His flight bag, bought new at the start of his career, was the only constant in his life, and its gradual decay marked the passage of his itinerant living until the point when it disintegrated and he knew it was time to stop. 'I loved that bag,' he says. Love! For a bag! But I know what he means.

I've bought a new biking bag now, a modern thing made by Alpinestars, a sort of 'by bikers, for bikers' type of thing. And, as with people who buy a new car only every twenty years and are astonished by electric windows, I'm amazed at how the backpack has come on. It's a better shape and more comfortable, being moulded closer to the spine's desire. It has better zips, more compartments, effective waterproofing, more easily adjustable straps, stronger material. It is a superior product in every single way.

Give me a couple of decades and I might even come to like it.

Triples all round

Regular readers may remember that, some weeks back, I promised myself a new Triumph Speed Triple motorcycle if I could throw three treble 20s on the local pub dartboard.

I'd been working reasonably hard, putting a bit aside, renouncing the devil that sat on my shoulder and taunted me with talk of stair carpet, and generally honouring my Protestant upbringing. Save now, spend later; neither a lender nor a borrower be, do not fall into the clutches of Mammon by buying on the tick.

Anyway, last week, on a particularly quiet Tuesday evening in the Cross Keys, I finally did it. Despite the new telly mounted on a wall bracket midway between the oche and the raddled blackboard, positioned only a few inches above the ideal treble-20 trajectory and therefore a bit off-putting, I was rewarded with the satisfying thunk of three arrows piercing the virgin red rectangle denoting the highest score on the board.

It's a pity that, as with so many holes-in-one and prize-winning pike, no one else was there to see it. I was the only customer. Even the landlady had temporarily disappeared into the cellar and, when she re-emerged a few seconds later, could only stare in disbelief at a grouping never before seen in the pub's 150-year history. There have been at least five previous boards since I've been a regular, and each has been committed to the skip in the sobering knowledge that the treble 20 has been a waste of good bristle.

What a great bike. Ugly and pugnacious, perhaps, but in a well-bred sort of way, like Raffles the Gentleman Thug in *Viz*. I'd forgotten what an appealing layout the transverse triple is. A single thuds, a V-twin clatters, and the ubiquitous in-line four simply blends with that aural backdrop that is all the four-cylinder cars out there. But the triple has a slight irregularity to it – a murmur of mechanical dissent, almost – which produces a fabulously resonant and gravelly exhaust note. It's like riding around on Lee Marvin.

The Trumpet has been declared by many reputable motorcycling magazines to be the best and most capable of the naked big-bore streetbikes. Mind you, the Slazenger racket owned by my schoolmate Lonny was generally regarded as the finest tennis weapon a 14-year-old could possibly be given by an ambitious parent. The notoriety he earned from having one was second only to that he enjoyed for his embarrassing incompetence on the tennis court.

Similarly, I once played saxophone in a jazz band that included a bloke called George, who had a rare and very valuable electric guitar. Everyone was very impressed with George's guitar, but rather less so with George's abilities on it. When the programme for our next gig was produced, it listed saxophonists, trombonists, a pianist and a bassist. But George appeared as a 'guitar owner'.

The fact remains that I'm still not really that good at riding motorcycles, and certainly nowhere near as good as my new bike would suggest. This is why I won't be campaigning the Speed Triple in this year's Thundersprint meeting. Once again, organiser Frank Melling* has cajoled me into taking part, mainly by filling in the forms on my behalf and then sending me my race number.

---

*Daily Telegraph classic motorcycling correspondent and accomplished cake decorator.

Yes, the Thundersprint is a race meeting, a sprint contest. You can find out all about it by looking it up on what in Frank's neck of the woods is known as 'tinternet'. The course is short and tortuous, and the hay bales are very close to the track. A torquey, short-wheelbase and famously agile bike like the Speed Triple ought to do quite well on it, having the grip to allow the rider to 'get it right over' (as Rocket Ron Haslam would say) and the grunt to power out of the bends and down the short straight sections. So if you owned a Speed Triple but couldn't actually ride it properly, the whole thing could have been designed with the express aim of making you look a right donkey and like a bloke with all the gear and no idea.

I've therefore entered my 1964 Honda 90, a bike with a top speed of around 45mph, perhaps twenty of which might be attained on the opening straight. Hopefully the good-natured weekend crowd will applaud the self-deprecation of the bloke with the comically small motorcycle and absurdly large crash helmet.

He'll come last, as usual, but then he would, wouldn't he? Look at his bike.

Rolls-Royce – no longer a car for clowns

I may have done a bad thing. Using man maths, I've bought a car, having put another of my cars up for sale, while assuming it's worth more than I'll actually get for it, obviously, because that's how the books balance.

And it's even worse than that, because the car I'm selling is my dearly beloved Bentley T2. The one I've already bought is a fixed-head Rolls-Royce Corniche. Not only has the Rolls cost more than I imagine the Bentley is worth; once I've factored in the real value of the Bentley I'll also have to contribute the money I think I still have from selling a Triumph motorcycle four years ago, even though I spent that on a piano.

According to one or two of my mates, however, the arithmetic is the least of my problems. 'What?' said one. 'A Rolls-Royce? Won't you look like an ageing northern comedian?' I hadn't really thought of that. In fact, I hadn't really considered the image issue at all.

Confining our investigation, for the moment, to the two cars in question, I think there is a good case for the Rolls. The Silver Shadow and T-series saloons always looked better with the rounded Bentley grille up front, even though that, and the shape of the bonnet, is the only difference between them. Somehow, though, the two-door Corniche, though very closely related, looks more proper with that scale model of the Parthenon on the nose. Can't explain why; it just does.

The colour scheme of the Corniche is better, too. It's finished in the colour of Fitou, and the interior is plain and covered with an indistinct pale-beige hide. Now I once met a man with a condition known as synaesthesia, for whom things that you or I might regard as having shape, colour or texture manifested themselves as tastes. All Peugeots tasted of old fabric, and he could never own a Porsche because they combined Marmite with bananas and made him feel unwell. I was never really able to grasp this until I saw the Corniche, which immediately invokes a cheese and wine evening of the contemporary era, which was 1972. The Bentley, from 1980, is light metallic blue with a blue-piped creamy cabin, so looks like one of the star cars in *Boogie Nights*.

But what of the broader question of this thing called 'brand image'? It's undoubtedly true that over the last few decades the Rolls-Royce marque has suffered something of an credibility problem. By the late 90s R-R had become so undeniably nouveau that there was a case for replacing Sykes' Spirit of Ecstasy mascot with a gilded figurine of one of the Jimmies Saville or Tarbuck. Bentley, through the use of turbochargers and by exploiting its race heritage stuff and alluding to chaps in taches, had been transformed into the carriage of choice for the discerning enthusiast, or something like that. But now I'm not so sure.

Let's get one thing absolutely straight: the toffs aren't buying either of them. They're all broke, and busy flogging the Rembrandts to pay off the staff and keep them quiet. Posh cars are bought by rap stars and new-media entrepreneurs, so there's no point in being hung up about breeding.

If anything, I reckon Bentleys have become the more bling of the two. The Continental GT is too cheap to be truly exclusive, and take a look at the wheels on the Arnage T. There's more rubber in the suspension of a 70s model. Rolls-Royce, now a separate concern again, looks a bit more louche and can be had with snakeskin-effect interior door panels. But Simon Cowell has one. Two, possibly. And apparently 50Cent had one and sawed the roof off.

So what have I actually done to my self-esteem by trading a Bentley for a Rolls-Royce? As it turns out, absolutely nothing. There's a huge amount of old cock talked about 'the badge' and 'the brand', but taking this sort of thing seriously is nothing more than an admission that you don't know what you're on about. What I actually admire, in the end, is cars that were built in the Crewe factory and its Mulliner Park Ward subsidiary. All Rolls-Royce and Bentley models of the 70s and 80s are exactly the same bar a few detail trim differences; they were made by the same people to the same standard, which was a very high one, and to imagine that each says something different about you is utterly facile. They say a great deal about their creators, not their owners. We are merely celebrating it.

As real aristocrats, when we still had them, were fond of saying: those who mind don't matter. And those who matter don't mind.

A modernist's guide to the Goodwood Revival

I realise I'm a bit late with this, but I wanted to say what a smashing time I and my car-bore chums had at this year's Goodwood Revival. Great cars stretching as far as the eye could see was pretty good in itself, but there were also eight Spitfires in the air at one time and, best of all, I finally had the chance, after some thirty-five years of waiting, to meet Raymond Baxter; a man who in my opinion, and for his commentary on the Farnborough Airshow alone, should be Sir Raymond Baxter and bar.

I've never been to the revival before, only the Festival of Speed. The Festival is a merely a series of timed romps up the (admittedly very long) driveway of Goodwood House, but the revival takes place on the circuit that nearly killed Stirling Moss and was eventually struck from the Grand Prix calendar for being too dangerous. And here were period cars on pathetic tyres racing for real in the pouring rain.

Of course it rained on the Saturday, but we're British, not Italian, and we don't care. As long as there are carrier bags our plucky public will stick them on their heads and shrug this sort of thing off. In any case, the rain made the racing more dramatic and, as Dr Johnson observed, 'When two Englishmen meet, their first talk is of the weather'. Some trite remark about a downpour is a great way to break the ice with a man about to drown in the cockpit of his 60s Formula One car.

I admit that there are some things about the revival that

make me nervous. It's themed, for example, which means dressing up in 40s and 50s clothing, and I've always believed that anything involving dressing up – such as working for McDonald's or being a high-court judge – should be avoided. Some parts of the infield looked like the set of *It Ain't Half Dad's Army Do 'Ave 'Em Mum*.

But at least it allows you to identify immediately all those who wish either that the war was still on or that they'd been born American, and avoid them instead. Someone pointed out that I'd got the decade wrong and come in 1970s gear, to which I had to point out, gently, that they were just my normal clothes.

The theme of the evening party was 'The Last Days of the Raj', which for most of us meant traditional Indian garb. I've always thought this sort of thing looks pretty pukka on real Indians, but on me and my pals it looked more like an episode of *Carry On Up The Costume Hire Shop*. Fortunately, no one in our party *was* Indian, thus sparing us from another embarrassing these-are-my-normal-clothes incident.

But the cars! C-types, D-types, old Alfas and Maseratis, even a Maybach (from 1946, not the current wheeled branch of Maplins Electronics). It is quite incredible to observe how machines that were once funded by whole industries have become the personal playthings of an old-car elite. The pits abound with toffs, playboys, and investment bankers, which could be exclusive and intimidating anywhere else. But because the heroically foppish Lord March is a gentleman and an egalitarian, we of the shoeless proletariat are allowed to wander the pits, examine and even touch things, and exclaim 'Eeh look at this one our Johnny isn't that a real smasher', or however it was people spoke during the Suez Crisis.

All of this, however, pales into nothingness alongside the achievements of the motorcyclists in the Barry Sheene Memorial Trophy, a celebration of racing bikes from the early 60s run in the pouring rain. They were not all young, and as Mike Haywood (not a bike racer, but Rotherham's own poet) said:

Old age strikes fast
Like rooted trees
And grabs these lads
Below the knees.

But it hadn't got to this lot yet. Superb camerawork on Goodwood's own TV system recorded the elegance with which they tipped Manx Nortons and Matchless G50s into the streaming Woodcote corner; the faultless fluidity of their arm- and legwork in the face of the threat of a certain spill if they got it wrong. I've never ridden any of these old race bikes, but my guess is that they're even trickier to ride than they are to start, and desperately unforgiving. It is often said that a modern car has ten times the computing power of an Apollo space rocket; here was a grid full of machines with less collective computing power than an electric doorbell. But, by crikey, these chaps could ride them.

As a notoriously wobbly motorcyclist, I realised I should be able to do better in the dry on a normal road on a thoroughly modern Yamaha. So the next day I went out, and I did.

That's what I liked most about this event. Revival my 1940s flat hat. It was more of an inspiration.

How the small car will save the car

It's now three years since I've been to the Frankfurt Motor Show, which sounds like a terrible lapse of professionalism but to be honest, I'm quite glad. The Frankfurt Show represents, by some margin, the longest walk a motoring journalist will ever take, and all for the purpose of looking at some cars. So it's not just knackering, it's also strangely ironic. One year, an unfortunate German correspondent actually died on the way round, it was all so gruelling.

For the last two years I've been tied up with the filming of *Top Gear*, and this year, at the last minute, I was required to be elsewhere to give a talk about my new book, *James May's 20th Century*, which I'm delighted to say is on special offer at Woolworths and some supermarkets and a rollicking good read to boot (people like Jilly Cooper get away with this sort of thing, so why shouldn't I?).

However, I sort of wish I'd made it this time, because it's clear from the musings of my colleagues at *Telegraph* Motoring that something is going on: small cars, small engines, small amounts of CO2, small performance and other things terribly unappealing to small boys, who are the only true and uncorrupted arbiters on such matters. It is beginning to look as though green concerns have finally triumphed, and that this fantastic petrol-soaked party we've been having over the last 100 years is finally winding down. The band is well into the smoochy numbers, some of the chairs have been stacked up, and now the lights are back on everything looks a bit shabby.

So I'm here to tell you not to worry yet. For a start, a lot of it has the ring of cant about it. Mercedes-Benz may talk a good DiesOtto or hydrogen fuel cell, but while no one's been looking they've managed to shoehorn their biggest V8 into the C-class, just to confirm that they haven't lost any of their well-established ability to overdo it. By the time you read this, I'll be driving it.

More to the point, and as I've tried to argue in my new book, *James May's 20th Century*, which is currently available at a discount from some supermarkets and far easier to digest than many products at twice the price, small, slow cars are more important than big, fast ones. Small cars are more fun for more of the people more of the time, and if they didn't exist, neither would the posh stuff.

Furthermore, and as I might have gone on to say in *James May's 20th Century** if I'd been this cross when I was writing it, building a small, low-priced, spacious, fuel-efficient and crash-worthy car is a much more testing engineering proposition than building a 500 horsepower supercar for £200,000. I can't actually prove this, but conversations with car engineers who have tried both suggest it's true. Every few years some nutcase with an old industrial unit announces that he is going to build the ultimate uncompromised megacar, because Ferrari and Porsche are somehow getting it all wrong. These people never attempt to build an £8000 80mpg city car. Why? Because that's far too difficult.

It amuses me, then, that the anti-car lobby and misguided ecologists think that they are sounding the death knell of any car more elaborate than my Fiat Panda. Nothing could be further from the truth. Public pressure and government initiatives to cap a manufacturer's overall across-the-range CO_2

---

*On special offer in Woolworths and some supermarkets.

output will almost certainly force the development of clever small cars, but as a result of that the whole business of car-making will be in ruder health than ever. If they can get those cars right, they can do anything, and when the small cars are good, the big ones tend to be better.

I could go further. In fact, I shall. I suspect that creating a truly fabulous car is a task best discharged by those who have proved themselves with stuff for the masses. It explains why Ford came to trounce Ferrari at Le Mans. Remember, too, that the Porsche 911 would never have existed without the Beetle before it, and that the automotive might of Japan was founded largely on K-class runabouts that were barely more sophisticated than the cyclecars of the 1920s.

Consider this: the fastest, rarest, most expensive and most technologically replete supercar to date has been built by a company that was named for the people's everyday need simply to get about. Of course, they bought another badge to put on it, but everyone knows that the Bugatti Veyron is a Volkswagen. And it's all the better for it.

Relax. Pour yourself another pint of petrol. It's not over yet.

Eee I 'ad one of them – best bike ever

In case anyone out there is about to move house, I'll share a theory of mine.

When you move, you pack everything you own into cardboard boxes and transport them to the new home. The really important stuff – the kettle, your pants, the tin opener, the piano – is all put in one 'essentials' box, which you will open immediately on arrival. But the rest of the boxes will be opened as and when.

And here's the thing. In my attic are several unopened packing cases. They are not, as you might imagine, ones that I haven't yet opened in the five years I've lived here. Oh no. They were never even opened in the last house. They came from the one before that.

I no longer have any idea what's in these boxes, but I'm fairly confident that it's nothing terribly important; nothing that, by its absence, is diminishing my lot in life. My tip for moving house, then, is this: any box that remains unopened after six months should be taken straight to Oxfam or the tip.

Sadly, and as Dr Johnson observed, no man practises so well as he writes. For some reason, my house remains cluttered with stuff that Steptoe and Son would have thrown away, while things that I valued deeply have been allowed to slip through my fingers.

In one cupboard, for example, is a set of aluminium saucepans I never used as a student, and which we now know would have left me brain-damaged had I done so. So if I still have these, how come I no longer own a Jaguar XJ6 Coupé?

The Jag was a casualty of one of those days (I'm sure everyone except Elton John has these) when I awoke to the realisation that there was too much stuff in my life. So I advertised the Jag on the devil's own website (eBay) and sold it for a pitiful and non-life-changing amount to some Dutch bloke.

Why? Here I sit, still in possession of my collection of 400 *Commando War Stories in Pictures* books, my dried-up oil paints and easel, my photographic developing tank and the half-finished lute I began in woodwork evening class. Clearly there was no room in my life for a mint and rare old Jaguar.

I knew immediately that selling it was a mistake, and was amazed at the magnitude of the regret I felt as the Dutchman drove away. Although not as amazed as I was when he rang, some seven hours later, to say he'd made it to the other side of Holland.

On another of these Black Dog days I decided that, among the train set, the George Formby grilling machine and the camping equipment, the thing that was really afflicting me with the burden of ownership was a Kielkraft kit of a Piper Super Cruiser I'd been given as a child but somehow never built. I'd noticed (eBay again) that unmade Kielkraft kits were fetching good money among collectors, so I extracted it from behind the disused wine rack and seized fishing rod and sold it for £35.

I have no sense now of how the £35 enhanced my life but I do know that there will never be a tender moment in retirement when I finally lift the lid on that pile of balsa and think, 'Right. At last . . .'.

What I really rue, though, is the day I sold my 1978 Moto Guzzi California. A few years back, I and my mate Colin rescued this bike from the back of a shed, where it had lain untouched since a man called Franco dumped it there, with just 4500 miles on the clock, in 1984.

Why I sold it I now don't know. I am at a loss to imagine how I opened the door of the garage and thought that, out of the pile of useful wood offcuts, stiff paintbrushes, spare tiles, plant pots, mouldy sports equipment, rusty barbecue sets and a broken clock, the California was the thing that would simply have to go. I almost wept as the buyer (yes, eBay) rode away.

And here, finally, is the rather selfish point I want to make. The other day, at a car show, I met someone who claimed to be a mate of the bloke who bought it. At first I was overjoyed to hear that a man who had ridden away on a bike whose brakes I had rebuilt was still alive. Then I was outraged to learn that he'd restored it, when I'd expressly forbidden it, even though it wasn't mine any more. Then I was told that it was for sale again.

I'd like it back, please. Steve, I think your name was, and you may have lived in Brighton. You can have top money and your choice of any mystery sealed box from anywhere in my house.

(Author's note: I have since bought the Guzzi back from Steve, at a truly enormous price. Good for him.)

The queen of clean

My Woman Who Does is an undeclared genius. For her, the dismissive title of 'cleaner' is not enough. In a just world she would appear on the back of a banknote as the Domestic Rampant, triumphant on top of a heap of vanquished bacteria, wielding one of the mysterious bottles of household cleaning product that live in the uncharted space below the sink; there to symbolise the victory of truth and lemon freshness over the all-pervading dust of the earth.

Consider my cooker – a little-used appliance, admittedly, but potential host to some of the vilest filth in creation. There are dark corners and crevices in the average cooker that remain inhabited by the demons of dirt from the day it's installed to the day it's dumped in the recycling yard. But not mine. My cooker will go to Kitchen Hell with a perfectly clean conscience, and when it is smelted in the eternal fire not a gram of the slag that rises to the surface will be formed from Spam fat or the fossilised breadcrumbs from fish fingers. You could eat your lunch off my cooker.

But how often should one have the home help in? Originally, she came on Monday for four hours, but that meant the house was only truly gleaming once every seven days. So now I have her twice a week for three hours at a time.

And on the face of it, that would appear to be too much cleaning. This is a modest house with only two permanent inhabitants, me and Fusker the cat. There are no children, so no sticky fingerprints on the doors and no wax crayons trodden in to the carpet. What's more, I'm often away for lengthy stretches but have my cleaner in anyway, with the result that I once returned home from a long trip to discover that the individual buttons of my desktop calculator had been cleaned. So had the buttons on the TV remote control.

On another homecoming from a lengthy absence, I opened my Cupboard of Plenty and found all the tinned and packet foodstuffs arranged in the order in which they would surpass their sell-by dates. Clearly, I have over-employed my cleaner.

Or have I? If I'm here, then in the three days between visits I can make a truly appalling pigpen of this place; not just by normal standards but, especially, by the very high standards in place immediately after her departure, when I hardly dare move. Cleanliness in the home is something I obviously value, so it should be clean all the time. I need her for one hour every day.

Then again, as I write I've only been in the house for a morning, and already there are several teacups on the floor, some crumbs in the kitchen and the remnants of my stubble in the sink. There's something not entirely inert in the shower. Really, I need her to follow me around at all times with a damp cloth.

If I hadn't employed a cleaner at all, none of this would bother me. The cack would have sort of neutralised at some point, like the corrosion on a cast-iron manhole cover. It would have been unsightly, but it wouldn't have got any worse. Instead, I have become neurotic about the one thing I can't achieve myself – cleanliness.

Which brings me to the point I'm trying to make, which is cleaning the car. Traditionally, the British clean the car once a week, on Sunday. But what's the point of that? As soon as it's used it will be dirty again, and after a week it will be plastered in muck. If a clean car is important – and it clearly is, or we wouldn't do it – it needs to be cleaned constantly. I now find myself cleaning the car almost as often as I use it.

But that's easy compared with the torment offered by a motorcycle. Motorcycles attract dirt like a divorce lawyer, and each one features thousands of included angles where grime and corruption can congregate in a matter of miles. My colleagues think I enjoy cleaning my bike, but nothing could be further from the truth. I loathe it. Unfortunately, I have come to loathe the dirt even more.

Cleaning the bike involves countless mysterious solutions, sponges, bits of rag and pointy things that will reach into corners. Just the sort of thing my daily is good at. So here's the problem.

I am a man of modest breeding and ambitions, and am therefore slightly uncomfortable with the idea of servants. Some of you, though, probably have staff and know perfectly well how to talk to them. So: is it acceptable to employ her indoors for another few hours a week, but this time in the garage?

More to the point, how do I put it?

Motoring holiday spoiled by tasteless curtains

Every year, somewhere on the planet, some sort of global association of caravan, camper van and mobile home manufacturers meets up for an annual conference at which it reaffirms its ongoing objective of lowering world standards of taste in interior design.

What other explanation can there be for the decor in the Monaco Dynasty motorhome I'm currently driving around California?

What's more, I think I have found the venue for this year's gathering. It's the Mount Madonna Country Park, Santa Clara, where the early-morning sun, fragmented by the overhanging leaves of huge and ancient sequoia trees, bursts through the windows and skylights of countless 'recreational vehicles' and dapples with perfectly golden light some of the worst cushions I've ever seen.

On the whole, I'm becoming quite fond of the RV. It's forty-two feet long, or four feet longer than the timeless Routemaster bus, and in Blighty I'm not sure I'd be allowed to drive it. Here, though, I simply had to sign a few forms, hand over the cash, and I was free to demolish whole housing estates.

In other guises, this vehicle would be able to transport two football teams or, in the wine-growing regions of Paso Robles, 500 Mexicans. Arranged as the Dynasty, it is expected to be home to just two people. Starting from the door, the visitor moves through the sitting room, the dining area and then the fully equipped kitchen, complete with American-style double-door fridge packed with flavour-free cheese and industrial bolognese sauce. Or at least until some idiot* leaves the special latch mechanism undone and it all falls out on a fast left-hander because the doors have opened. Through a sliding door is the bathroom and the small room that Americans call the 'bathroom'.

Open another sliding door to reveal the master bedroom, with wardrobes, laundry room and king-size double bed. It's pretty accommodating as it is, but when parked up, the sides of the whole rig can be made to expand outwards to double the floor area. It boasts two home cinemas, is the biggest vehicle I've ever driven on a public road and the only one equipped with a doorbell. I imagine this was what it was like being in Led Zeppelin.

But, obviously, I have a few complaints. One is that every few days the 'black tank' and the 'grey tank' have to be emptied at special RV waste stations. Essentially, the grey tank holds all the waste water from showering and washing up (i.e. not much) and the black tank is full of Oz Clarke's number twos (i.e. bursting).

Another is this. At proper trailer parks full of banjo-playing Republicans the rig can be hooked up to a mains electricity supply, just as a regular caravan might be. Elsewhere, though, it relies on a small generator housed in its nose and which must be run constantly if the white Zinfandel in the fridge is to remain at a constant and acceptable temperature. This does not bother the wine bore in his luxury suite aft, but as I don't like him in that way I sleep on the floor or the sofa in the sitting room, some thirty feet for'ad. It's not the most refined diesel engine in the world so I feel as though I've been sleeping with my head resting against one of those yellow roadside generators – you know the sort of thing I mean; the ones that run

---

*Me, to be honest

all night for the purpose of powering a small yellow lamp that's been nicked by some students anyway.

Finally, there is the all-important issue of the furnishings. What in the name of the almighty were the creators of the Dynasty thinking of? The television series? Given the holiday remit of what is really a very large camper van, I would expect something of a holiday atmosphere on board; that is, simple, bright and cheerful colours, gaily patterned curtains, bold and functional design and wipe-down materials everywhere.

Instead, the Dynasty is a paean to the brown end of the colour spectrum. Fixed furniture is upholstered in ruched tan leather, the soft ones are sculpted dark-brown and brick, the carpet is a dark brown leaf motif on a pale brown background and the curtains are beige.

The extensive fitted cupboards are some sort of mahogany with baroque relief carvings, the handles are pseudo-bronze and the worktops and table are fashioned from polished cream Italian terrazzo with a hint of coffee granule. For a vehicle intended as a place of recreation and leisure, it really is over-whelmingly institutional.

Whoever is in charge of global motorhome interior design policy needs to realise that until this issue is sorted out, camper-vanning is never going to be truly acceptable. Apart from anything else, you're ruining my holiday. Every time I climb aboard I think I've come to see someone about my overdraft.

A balanced view on the irrelevance of handling

I know this is going to sound like a slightly pompous thing to say, but a shotgun with 28-inch barrels really does feel very different from one with 30-inch barrels.

It's all to do with the inertia of the thing, which affects how quickly and easily you can swing it around.

Similarly – no, not similarly, actually, but illustrative of the same point – a heavy wooden ladder, carried horizontally, is much harder to manoeuvre than a lightweight aluminium one, even if they are the same length. The issue is still inertia, but this time as a result of weight and its distribution.

How bloody boring is this? Fairly, I'd say, and no doubt you're expecting me to continue with an explanation of why the mid-engined layout is good for handling, and why the Lancia Stratos was so successful as a rally car because it was both mid-engined and short.

And I was, until I thought about it all a bit harder, and then I decided that handling is actually a bit pointless. I've realised, too, that every time I arrive at a bit of a road test that talks about tread shuffle or balancing it on the throttle or how the car can be gathered up with an armful of opposite lock, I put the magazine down and find something more constructive to do, such as texting the Old Testament to someone.

Come on, who really cares about this stuff? A while back we entered a 24-hour motor race at Silverstone in a modified BMW 3 Series diesel, and even I could see that handling was sort of relevant around the track – the way it turned under braking, for example, or the benign onset of its understeer in that corner I call 'Abbey' because it has an Abbey National hoarding next to it, but which is really Copse. Or Vale.

But on the track everyone was going in the same direction, even me, and it didn't really matter if you crashed. Out in the real world, though, handling simply isn't important.

Now I accept that, on a subliminal level, handling is a good thing. I think the Lotus Exige is a nice handling car, but not in the way that a man with bad sunglasses does. I simply like the crisp precision of the thing, and the alertness of its responses. But I have never been seen turning its wheel the wrong way in a corner.

I also like the way my Boxster feels in a tight corner; the way it hunkers down and the steering weights up slightly. But not in the way a man who sits too close to the wheel might like it. You know the sort I mean – arms bent, steely-eyed stare fixed straight ahead, looking for the next opportunity to 'exploit the chassis'. Precision haircut. Nobber.

Elsewhere, though, I've taken a bit of a stand against handling. For years I also tooled around in an old 1980 Bentley saloon that had been fitted with something called the Harvey Bailey Handling Kit. This firmed it up and improved its composure etc etc. But I never really approved of it, because it spoiled the ride, so I became the first man in history to book my car into a workshop with the complaint that it handled too well.

The solution, it turned out, was not to remove the handling kit but to get rid of the car altogether, and replace it with a 1972 Rolls-Royce Corniche. Back in 1972 a Rolls-Royce wasn't actually fitted with handling, in the way that the L version of a family saloon was not fitted with a radio or clock. In fact, I like to believe that if you worked for R-R back then and ever used the 'H' word, you'd have been locked in the stockroom until you learned some manners.

The net result of all this is highly entertaining. The steering

wheel of the Corniche simply provides directional sugges-
tions rather than actual input, as if it's fulfilling a sort of
non-executive role in the whole business, or is just too damned
polite to issue an actual instruction. It seems fine on a straight
road, and after a while I find myself driving one-handed. Then,
after a while longer, I'm driving one-handed and with my elbow
on the armrest. Then I just have a forefinger and thumb clasping
the rim and finally, well into the journey when I've been lulled
into a sense of plutocratic torpor, I resort to a single pinkie
hooked lightly over its Bakelite magnificence.

And that's when, suddenly and for no apparent reason, it
dives into the ditch at the edge of the road like a refugee during
an air strike. It's hilarious.

Tell me that getting an Evo sideways is more fun than that.

First class super saver day return – by Fiat

One thing that has always bothered me about train travel – and I know I'm not alone in this is why it costs so much more at peak times.

Surely it should be cheaper? It's more crowded, and therefore less savoury. There's less chance of finding a seat and, even if you do, more chance that you'll find yourself among some marketing executives having a meeting. There's a good chance, too, that the trolley service will run out of fruitcake. And yet for this, we are expected to pay a premium.

A man who knows about trains explained it thus: higher prices at busy times helps subsidise the trains during quiet parts of the day, when there are fewer passengers. This is ridiculous. I have to pay a fortune to be annoyed by a man with a bleeping laptop when, a few hours later, pensioners and the workshy can pay a few pence to travel in their own private carriages, like Hermann Goering, with more fruitcake than they can hope to consume in one lifetime. I've a good mind to write to OffFob.

But this is nothing compared with my bafflement the other day upon attaining my seat on the 0800 London to Edinburgh service at King's Cross, hoping to alight at York. 'Hi everyone,' said a manly voice over the Tannoy system. 'My name's Gary and I'll be travelling with you today.'

For one horrible moment I thought I'd boarded a special train run by an organisation for people who had difficulty in coming to terms with some embarrassing personal issue. I thought perhaps all the passengers would have to stand up and give short introductory speeches before publicly confronting whatever it was they hated about themselves. But then I realised that he was what in the old days – that is, when one simply went to 'the station' and got on 'the train' – would have been called 'the guard'.

He went on to explain some of the restrictions that applied to tickets on this particular train. If I understood him correctly, Saver tickets were not valid, but Business Saver tickets were. Standard and First Class tickets must be used on the correct train otherwise a new ticket must be purchased from him, in what used to be called the 'guard's van'. My ticket appeared to be valid, unless it was an FCC ticket. I'd know if it was, because it would say FCC in the bottom right-hand corner. But he didn't explain what FCC meant.

There was more. Restrictions on the Scottish leg of the journey were different, and there was something that only applied to Peterborough. Certain conditions applied between Peterborough and York, but not, it seemed, if you boarded in London and stuck it out until Edinburgh. Some passengers could get off in York but only if they got off in London first and waited for a later service. This went on for what seemed like hours.

I think it may have been possible for an Englishman and a Scotsman to sit alongside each other with the same type of ticket but evolve into a bad joke because the Scotsman couldn't get off in England but the Englishman could go to Scotland. But not if he'd got on in Doncaster before 0900.

It was truly absurd. I'm all for capitalism and privatisation, but only so long as it doesn't become boring. This was almost enough to drive me to Marxism. Instead, however, I thought, 'sod this for a game of trains. It would be easier to buy a small car'. So a couple of days later I did just that.

Several things provoked this. First of all, I really like simple, small cars. I've owned several Minis and a Citroën Visa, and found myself yearning once more for those prosaic qualities that come with basic motoring. I'd also finally sold my aged Range Rover, which had a moonshot mileage and was creeping inexorably into that twilight period between dependability and needing a bit of work.

Then I remembered that a good mate owed me a lump of money I'd lent him a while back when his Switch card had been stolen. Finally, I realised that over the last year I had inadvertently saved up enough money for the posh stair carpet I've been promising myself, which meant it must be time to spend it on something more interesting. Before I knew it, I had enough for a new Fiat Panda. And, believe me, compared with buying something like a train ticket it is joyously easy to buy a Fiat Panda.

The experience also seems to confirm something that I've long maintained; that the future of transport, whatever form it takes, will be something personal, not public.

How the three-day week improved your car

Last Sunday, I was driving an Austin Princess from 1978. *Top Gear* were investigating, on the fortieth anniversary of its creation, whether or not British Leyland ever made a good car.

Obviously, making the case for the Princess was always going to be difficult in the face of unrelenting Terry and June gags from the other two idiots, but the more I thought about it, the more I realised that the cheese-derived big Austin was actually pretty commendable. What really impressed me, though, was how good it looked. I'm going to take the bold step of declaring the Princess to be a fine piece of automotive design – worthy of Alfa Romeo from the front.

Jeremy's Rover SD1 looked good as well. In fact I'll be bolder still, and risk the opprobrium of the wood 'n' leather lobby by saying that some of the most memorable and arresting designs in British car history came from the 1970s: the Princess, the Jaguar XJ-S, the Aston Martin Lagonda, the Rolls-Royce Camargue, the Reliant Scimitar GTE and – and this is the tricky one – the Triumph TR7. Yes, I think the TR7 was a great-looking car. We thought it was at the time and it still is.

Let me make absolutely clear that I'm not recommending any of these things. As cars, British cars of the 70s were not terribly successful. It must have been difficult to build a car properly when so much of your time had to be devoted to stoking a brazier and buying donkey jackets. Making cars is a full-time job. And they weren't all lookers. The Maxi may have been a wonderful exercise in space utilisation but it looked bloody boring, and the Allegro seems to have been inspired not so much by the space race as by the space hopper. But the good stuff was very, very good. It was as if every established tenet of car design had been cast aside and stylists were as delirious as a released prisoner in a pub; as if someone had heeded Tennyson's warning that one good custom would corrupt the world.

Let's return to the TR7. The TR6 obviously owed a lot to the TR5, and so on back through the whole canon of TR sports cars. But the 7 came from nowhere, and looked completely new in every way. It also, I will maintain, looked fabulous. Likewise the Rover SD1. Every Rover before it had been signed off by a bank manager, but here was a hatchback with a box for a dashboard and styled to look like a Ferrari. The XJ-S retained none of the stylistic language that defined what a Jaguar should be in the minds of fools in old-style hats and coats, as Larkin put it, and the Lagonda was so outrageously freestyle that it still looks modern today. It was all fabulously optimistic and forward-looking for an age when the electricity was only on half the time.

How did this happen? From what I remember of being a boy in the 70s, the news – when the telly was on, anyway – had a whiff of revolution about it. People are always telling me that the 60s was the era when society was redefined, but I can't help feeling that was just a lot of cheesecloth, casual sex and jazz cigarettes. In the 70s, it was serious, and somehow or other it was recorded in the profile of my Princess. You couldn't go ten yards without being frustrated by a protest or a picket line. The old order really was changing, and the past and everything in it was reviled. And I'm afraid that included Inspector Morse's MkII. The Beatles were just a bit stoned, but The Jam were very cross about something.

Somehow or other, this social tension gave us great-looking cars, in a way that the complacency of the mid-90s didn't. It probably helped that the stultifying cod science of marketing hadn't really been invented yet, and that car design was the work of one or two people with genuine convictions, but that doesn't explain it entirely. I wonder if someone like Simon Schama could demonstrate that great-looking cars come from societies in the process of reinventing themselves.

Since we're not reinventing ourselves very radically at the moment, it seems unlikely that there will be a really shocking British car design any time soon. But there is hope. Jaguar is about to launch the XF, the first radical departure from Jaguar saloon design since the 60s. It looks good; modern, stylish, unencumbered by the misplaced desire to plunder 'design heritage'. But it's still no XJ-S.

What's needed is a bit less what-the-customer-wants and a bit more Wat Tyler.

Mercedes-Benz, now you're just being silly

This may be an unfashionable view, but I'm absolutely certain it's not the job of government, at any of its levels, to tell me how to live.

In recent years, for example, there has been a government poster campaign advising me to keep an eye on my salt intake. We've had the *Manual for Streets* (see page 73), a sort of Strength Through Joy handbook to encourage us to socialise, plus various campaigns to provide guidance on how to bring up your children. Near me, the local mayor has spent millions of pounds of my money on posters extolling the virtues of walking and living a greener lifestyle.

Apart from anything else, I can work all this stuff out for myself. What I can't do is sort out the pensions crisis or the NHS. This is where big government, in the pompous building in Westminster, comes in. They are here to do the nation's admin, instead of foisting it upon the individual through devious means such as self-assessment income tax and deregulation of the phones business. At a local level, government's job is to make sure the bins are emptied and to put up some more park benches if enough people say they want them.

Even so, in May's Britain it's going to be hard to resist passing a few laws that, I know, will make life better for everyone. The first will be a blanket ban on any two-stroke engine of 50cc and under and, what's more, it will be retrospectively applied so that anyone owning a small scooter, a Flymo or a strimmer will have to hand the offending item in to the authorities for immediate recycling into a three-cylinder Triumph engine block. No one can argue that the country won't be better off without these things.

Here's another: this morning I saw a small poster announcing that I can earn up to £500 a month by displaying an advert on my car. London taxi drivers already do this, and adverts spoiled the fine and functional lines of the Routemaster bus over its entire service life. Now we are threatened with the spectre of a small electric car driving around town emblazoned with an official edict to the people to live better lives, i.e. communism. And where would it end? As aeroplanes sometimes pass quite close to my house, I can presumably have the Bile Beans logo writ large upon the roof and earn a few extra bob. Pretty soon England would look like the tinned food section of Sainsbury's, and we can't have that, so I won't allow it. You'll have a blue car and be grateful.

And I'm sorry, but I'm going to outlaw the Mercedes GL. Having spent a day driving it back and forth across the capital, I've decided that it really is too big, too excessive and, as my mother might say, totally unnecessary. Try as I might, I cannot think of a reason why anyone would buy one of these. If you want space you're better off with the R-class, if you want true luxury you're better off with the S-class, and if you genuinely want off-road ability you'd be in prison in May's Britain anyway.

It's not that it's big per se; I like big cars and have one. I'm in favour of extravagance, too, because it is the human right of a free people. But when it becomes wanton, it's somehow distasteful. I can't help feeling that with cars like the GL we are adopting an American approach to motoring, which means we really will end up with an obesity problem brought on largely, as it is over there, by too much cheese.

The GL feels like a clumsy approach to building a luxury car. Everything about it, from the screen pillars to the depth of the seat squabs, is big, thick-limbed and lumpen. All-round visibility is not that great, which makes it hard to use in town despite what someone somewhere has undoubtedly said about the commanding driving position. Its bigness doesn't yield much in the way of accepted big-car qualities. It just yields bigness.

Physically, it's burdensome, and psychologically it's a burden too. It would be forgivable if, out on the open road, it turned into something delightful, but it doesn't. Even equipped with the huge (and otherwise excellent) 5.5-litre V8, it isn't that fast. Meanwhile, around town, the effort of piloting it around, manoeuvring it through traffic and trying to park it is just a constant worry.

And it's not as if we haven't already got enough to worry about. Apparently quite a few of us have been drinking wine for years, without realising that it might make us a bit drunk.

The curse of carbon

When you sneeze, particles of snot can exit your nose at up to 50mph. That's the official and scientific belief, anyway. Sadly, because this is a good pub fact the true velocity of nasal egress has been exaggerated over time, and now people will happily tell you that a bogie can reach Mach 3.4.

Some years ago, somebody, somewhere (but almost certainly on Radio 4) pointed out that it was essential to drink water every day. He or she was probably a doctor or dietician, an authority of some sort, and was undoubtedly right.

Whoever it was also suggested a quantity for daily consumption, and I suspect it was something like 'two glasses' or 'half a litre'. I can't remember drinking more than that throughout my whole childhood, and I'm still alive and not drying up around the edges.

Sadly, though, this bit of wisdom made it to the pub somewhere and thus turned into folklore, with the result that it's been embellished. In the retelling, by the sort of people who love to say 'Your mouth is actually the dirtiest part of your body', the recommended daily intake has grown, until you'd now be forgiven for thinking that you'll die unless you drink a gallon of water every hour.

The cult of water drives me up the wall. On TV shoots people now come up to me, after I've completed maybe three minutes of talking to a camera, and say 'Do you need a water?' I've never 'needed' a water. T.E. Lawrence went across the Sinai peninsula on half a canteen of the stuff, so why would I need some after talking briefly? On a train last week the man in the buffet car announced over the Tannoy that he was selling tea, coffee, a range of sandwiches and 'a selection of waters'. There has never been a selection of waters, only water. And no one actually needs any at all.

Which doesn't really bring me to carbon fibre at all, but sort of does in a way, because it, too, is being foisted upon us when we don't really need it.

Yes yes yes yes I know I know I know: it makes sense for racing-car tubs, aeroplane wings, the shafts of golf clubs and fishing rods. But I'm talking here about carbon fibre as an adornment, which you will find in your car and other inappropriate places. I'm driven to this by the discovery that the carbon-fibre roof of the new BMW M3 is standard and not painted, so everyone can see it. Why?

What we tend to refer to as carbon fibre is usually, in fact, carbon-fibre-reinforced plastic, or CFRP, or CRP if you think 'carbon fibre' is one word, which I don't. On the face of it, it's a great material. It weighs roughly 1800kg per cubic metre, which compares well with mild steels at around 7800kg per cubic metre. Aluminium alloys weigh in somewhere in the 2600kg region. So carbon fibre really is very light.

However, no one is driving around with a cubic metre of steel in the car and lamenting its devastating impact on handling. Obviously, a carbon-fibre roof will lower the centre of gravity a bit, but so will having a haircut or removing the loose change from your pocket. It doesn't matter but does make you look a bit of a berk.

If you make the whole body shell out of the stuff – Enzo, for example – then it makes a significant difference. The downside, though, is that it's difficult to paint. Worse, once you've had a few you might inadvertently tell people that your car is made of carbon fibre, and then they'll think you're a big chump.

Because the true worth of carbon fibre has been debased by

its use as a sort of phoney high-tech jewellery it has become a fashionable trim material, and fashion is bollocks. Carbon-fibre dashboard, carbon-fibre pedals, carbon-fibre instrument faces – none of this is a legitimate engineering application of the stuff, it's just drawing attention to yourself. You can buy stick-on carbon-fibre sheets for motorcycle frames. I don't care how light it is, this must surely be adding unnecessary weight.

There are carbon-fibre pens, carbon-fibre carving-knife handles, carbon-fibre mobile phones, carbon-fibre briefcases. None of this stuff was ever deemed too heavy, was it? What am I to make of a man with a carbon-fibre briefcase? That he's deeply in touch with the technological zeitgeist? Or that he has consumption and can't lift a leather one?

I'm reminded of the early-80s elevation of the word 'turbo' to denote excellence in everything. The Saab Turbo was a cool car, therefore turbos were, and it was a short step from that to turbo vacuum cleaners, turbo sunglasses and turbo disposable razors. It's all nonsense.

Drink beer. Drive a metal car. Don't be a ponce.

The two most boring men in Britain

Last year, for BBC2, I made a programme called *Oz and James's Big Wine Adventure*. It was a simple idea, really. I would travel around France with a very old man called Oz Clarke, he would reveal the mystery and wonder of the grape to me, wean me off the bitter in my local, and turn me into a Chablis-sipping sophisticate able to hold my own at any level of polite drinking society.

Obviously it didn't work. For a start, almost everyone we met in France was French, and therefore something of a communist. The whole business of French wine is deliberately obscure and organised in such a way that the rural grape-growing population is locked in the Middle Ages, so it was all bloody donkeys and smocks and methods used by Pierre in 1350.

But I like to think of myself as a post-Enlightenment member of the industrial world, and I believe in the power of large-scale production to improve my life. Take the example of the car. The BMW Z4 coupe is doubtless the deeply creative work of people whose muses may be the same as those that inspired the cave painters of the Stone Age, but because we live in the age of manufacturing, it is a completely repeatable artefact, which is what makes it accessible to so many people. All BMW Z4 coupes are the same, which is exactly as we want it.

If this is possible with something as complicated as a car, it ought to be a piece of cake with a bottle of wine, surely? The French don't want to acknowledge it, because they like to think that the wine is something only they could possibly understand; that if the butcher from the nearby village farts in the direction of the vines on a windy day the bouquet will be subtly and uniquely altered, thus increasing its cultural and fiscal value.

This brings me to California, where I am currently making Oz and James series two. It was my idea to come here, because I believed that the amateur wino would be better served by the US than by any other nation on earth. In France, everything is unpredictable, as it is on an old Citroën. But in California the terrain, the weather, the workforce, the growing season, the bottling plant and the economy are all minutely understood, and so making consistent wine on a grand scale should come naturally to these people. It was the US that popularised things that in the old world seemed unequivocally elitist – the pocket watch, the motor car, the domestic refrigerator, the quarter pounder with cheese. I could rely on these people to make me a decent drop of consistent quality at a reasonable price. Bingo!

And they can. Two Buck Chuck makes his California Chardonnay for a pound a bottle, and it's really not at all bad. More to the point, it's always the same. He makes his wines in huge mechanised factories that look more like coking plants than the vision of timeless bucolic innocence we expect in Burgundy. Yet the stuff is perfectly drinkable, and no more expensive than real ale. It works for me. Oz Clarke, however, is not entirely convinced.

And now we arrive at the fundamental difference between us. With the best will in the world, I'm just a bit of a drunk and believe that the function of alcohol is to help shy and possibly ugly people to have sex. But Oz is actually a wine enthusiast and connoisseur. He likes to look at gravel in vineyards. He likes to stand on a hill and think about how the wind and temperature dictate the rate of grape-ripening and the effect that has on fruit flavours and acidity. He likes wine labels, wine corks and the boxes wine is shipped in, and knows everything about them. He can happily take out a bottle of rare wine, stand it on the table and just look at it. Oz Clarke is, by any normal person's standards, a wine bore.

And the tragedy of it all is this: that in his 120-year-old face I see a tragic mirror of myself, another bore, just abandoned in a different subject. One of the wine makers we visited drove an old Citroën DS, and I discovered I could talk about it uninterrupted for nearly half an hour. By the end of it, I'd driven the other bloke to drink.

Oz Clarke is amazed and outraged that people can be satisfied with a formulaic industrial wine that holds no surprises whatsoever. But it's only a ruddy drink, for Pete's sake. Then again, it still staggers me that so many people can sleep peacefully at night knowing that they own mid-size MPVs with diesel engines. But they're only cars. Most people couldn't give a toss about either.

And at least if you drink, you can forget.

Small electrical fault, would suit enthusiast

Yesterday, I was required to install a new wall-mounted light fitting in a small room in my house. There's nothing too difficult about this: a few holes in the wall, some Rawlplugs, and a bit of basic wiring. Brown is live, blue is not, green and yellow earth the lot.

That's right, isn't it?

In case I'd got it wrong, I turned the whole lighting circuit off. And then, in case the original electrician had got that wrong as well, I turned the whole house off, thus condemning myself to a day of resetting 101 clocks and timers. Then I reached for my most trusted tool, my old electrician's screwdriver; the sort whose handle lights up if the tip encounters anything live.

And it didn't light up when it touched the brown wire sticking out of the wall. Or the blue one. But how could I be sure the screwdriver still worked? To be on the safe side, I turned the house on again and stuck it in a light socket known to function. It lit up. Good. Turn the house off again.

Even at this point – and I realise this is idiotic – I brace myself, extend my index finger and touch the end of the live wire very very very quickly. Why? Electricity flows at the speed of light, and the speed of my finger is like the growth of a stalactite in comparison. But I somehow imagine it will hurt less that way.

I don't like electricity. I know it is the light of the world, but as a science, it dwells in darkness. Before all the usual teachers write in, I'd like to establish that of course I understand electricity in the broader sense. I know Ohm's Law, I am aware of the difference between voltage and current, and I can see how the flow of current in a simple DC circuit is analogous to the flow of water in a pipe. I can even explain why electricity distribution over large distances is more efficient using AC and transformers, and even Thomas Edison got that one wrong.

But despite this, I have never, from childhood onwards, been able to develop any sort of electrical intuition. I have never sensed an innate understanding in the very fibres of my being, as I do when confronted with a wonky mechanical clock or a sticky Sturmey-Archer three-speed bicycle hub. Electrical tasks fill me first with dread and then, inevitably, with electricity itself.

This, surely, explains why, whenever I dabble in the world of old cars, I come to grief over some aspect of their electrics. It will not have escaped the notice of avid *Top Gear* viewers that whenever the three of us compete in one of our old-car challenges, I always end up with something like a flat battery, a dead starter or an ignition issue. It's never a big-end failure or a gasket or a brake seizure.

But then, it wouldn't be, because I like to think I am imbued with a certain amount of mechanical sympathy. I can nurse a slipping clutch or a disintegrating gearbox for hundreds of miles, because I can feel their components at work and know how to minimise their mechanical trauma. But I can't do this with the electrical system. It is abstract, it provides no feedback, and it is nought more than sorcery.

However, it's not quite as simple as that. After thinking about this for a while, I've realised that nothing electrical in my life quite works properly: my computer printer, the central heating controller, the TV remote control, my mobile phone, my fax machine. Light bulbs always blow when I turn them on, digital watches turn to rows of eights when I wear them. My satnav went blank last week and the igniter on my gas cooker works for Woman but not for me.

I'm not prone to superstition, but there's definitely something spooky going on at the interface between me and the electric universe. It's not just a lack of comprehension, it's a Jonah-like influence. My mate Colin reckons that because my garage is integral with the house I am unwittingly sleeping above my Moto Guzzi in direct contravention of the rules of automotive feng shui. During the night, the ague-ridden vapours given off by the suspect Italian wiring soak into my bones, thus imbuing me with an aura of electrical malfunction that corrupts any device I go near.

This, finally, explains the failure of last week's *Top Gear* Reliant Robin space shuttle. Yes, it was only one bolt that prevented the orbiter separating from the main tank, but it was an explosive bolt, and the small black-powder charge designed to release it was triggered by the on-board electronics.

And I was standing within half a mile of it.

Brochure rage, part II

THE STORY SO FAR: Your humble correspondent has been consumed by brochure rage following a series of incidents in which the promotional literature accompanying everyday goods has been blighted by an excess of lifestyle imagery over product information. Or something like that. Now he has picked up the brochure for the new Aston Martin V8 Vantage Roadster. Read on . . .

I settled into the comfortable and squalid privacy of my home office, poured a hospital-sized measure of scotch, and prepared to indulge my fantasy of Aston Martin ownership.

However, when I opened the booklet at random, I thought some wag had glued a copy of *Hello!* between its inviting hard-backed and cloth-bound covers. Where's all the stuff about the car? More to the point, who's this ponce? And what's with the bird in the rich-bitch sunglasses? Surely there must be a caption beginning 'Marcus wears . . .'

But no. It must be the work of Aston Martin because there are some pictures of the Vantage Roadster. Sometimes it's out of focus in the background of one of the scenes that make up the pictorial narrative of the work, which seems to be about two beautiful people getting to know each other. Sometimes it isn't there at all. One spread is devoted to a portrait of her flouncing along a beach waving a scarf like Isadora ruddy Duncan. No mention of the power output, though (it's 380bhp in case, like me, you really were wondering).

Elsewhere, he is seen stubbly and moody in the driving seat, looking off-camera, his eyes exhibiting that far-off and distracted glaze seen only in those of men wracked by unrequited love and who wonder if she loves him or she loves him not. If he doesn't look where he's going it will become irrelevant. He will plunge off the edge of the remote Icelandic road along which he is supposedly driving, and the resulting airbag detonation may disfigure the classically proportioned nasal bridge that doubtless earned him the role in the first place. So – top speed? Sorry.

As the photo love story progresses, the two become plainly more intimate. They lean awkwardly against the boot lid, too bashful to look each other in the face, fearful of provoking the crouching tiger of true love. Instead, they have a little dance on some clifftops. Eventually, on the final page, we arrive at a monochrome portrait of the two taken a fraction of a second before they consummate their desires in the act of snogging. It's absolutely bloody disgusting. All the stuff about the car is printed in dense type on sugar paper in the back of the book.

I accept that I may be terribly out of touch here. Even so, I can't help wondering what a small boy – the motor industry's harshest critic – would make of the Aston brochure if he'd managed to nick one from the Earls Court Motor Show. He'd sit at home wondering if the whole event had just been a surreal dream, or if he'd accidentally gone to the What Not To Wear roadshow. It's not as if he'd come away with anything about cars.

It's interesting to compare Aston's efforts with the similar booklet that was my first tentative step towards buying a Porsche. It features a nice picture of the flat-six engine, just sitting there against a plain background, and on the following page a superb cutaway of it, so I can see how it works. There are also pictures of brake calipers and wheel options. There's even a picture of the exhaust catalyst. There is a coloured graphic to explain the use of different materials in the body structure, a schematic of the engine management system, and lovely graphs showing the power and torque outputs.

Crikey. I've just noticed another graph, showing the effect of the 'sport' button on throttle response in relation to pedal pressure. Cor! There are no people anywhere in this book, but at least when a chapter is headed 'model range' you know it will be about variations in the car. 'The Vantage Roadster is a unique and singular design statement,' says Aston Martin's brochure. Porsche's says 'The twin plenum chambers are connected via parallel pipes, one of which houses a valve.' No wonder the spine's falling apart.

I think I know how Aston's marketing consultancy was thinking: that the experience of car-buying needs to be liberated from the nerdy domain of the petrolhead, that women buy as many cars as men, and perhaps that the V8 Vantage must be seen as part of a total lifestyle experience.

But I couldn't care less. Cars are boring. Car enthusiasts are boring. I'm boring. I like a boring brochure.

That's why I drive a boring Boxster. Great car.

The Bentley in outer space

So – is the universe a solid? It's an interesting question, and one we shall return to in a moment, just as soon as I've told you about the office day trip to Jodrell Bank.

As a schoolboy – and who didn't visit Jodrell Bank as one? – we thought the place was fabulous. One friend spent his time there trying to calculate how many normal bowls of cornflakes it would take to fill the dish of the massive Mark 1A telescope, and how long it would take to eat them. Jodrell Bank was just a great day out, an excursive institution like the Tower of London, and no one really cared that in the vastness of space a lifetime travelling at the speed of light would get you pretty much nowhere.

But as an adult, I find that Jodrell Bank can be rather depressing. Space is so very, very big, and as hopeful mortals we find all that bigness rather damaging to our planetary self-esteem. In fact, our sense of place in the stellar scheme of things has been taking a regular beating ever since Copernicus postulated that we were not at the centre of everything, but rather just one of several useless lumps of space debris orbiting the sun. Then William Herschel reckoned to have mapped the whole of heaven, but in truth got no further than my garden gate, relatively speaking. Even then, space looked quite sizeable.

Enter Edwin Hubble, who realised that our own vast galaxy was merely one of countless thousands, most of them so distant that they look to us like single stars. Not only that, but he also realised that the whole thing was getting bigger by the minute, so we are being diminished in significance even as you read. We are but one speck of space dust in the great cosmic Hoover bag. Possibly less.

Still, all this must, statistically, increase the chances of other life. Well, I'm sorry to disappoint you, but my host at Jodrell Bank has been listening out there for forty years, and in all that time has heard nothing to suggest that we are anything but alone. Nothing. Not a peep. Not even the faint vestige of an intergalactic transmission of *The Archers* in Vulcan. He has calculated, in a bored moment when no Martians were logged on for him to talk to, that all the radio energy ever received by the giant Jodrell Bank dish would merely light the bulb from a pocket torch for a few seconds.

So here we are, unutterably lost in a space so incomprehensibly enormous that contemplating it without suffering serious and heart-chilling depression demands a new way of thinking. And so to a wall chart at the observatory that, like so much at the fuzzy edge of human comprehension, posed a question instead of providing a reassuring answer: 'Is the universe a solid?'.

Well, the view out of the window and my experience in aeroplanes suggests not. Then again, I remember a smug physics teacher telling me that solid matter is actually comprised largely of the gaps between the constituent parts of its atoms, and that if these were removed then the whole of Manchester would fit in a wardrobe, or something. So I have banished space-related misery with the thought that the entire universe is actually just part of the molecular structure of somebody's watch strap.

And the attempt to comprehend space – and this is a connection too tenuous even for James Burke – has at least allowed me to counter two objections to the Bentley Arnage T I've been driving this week; one my own, one other people's.

I've always loved the Arnage: its stance, its solidity, the meticulous detailing of its cabin. I have watched it mature from something slightly English Heritage and powered by BMW to something contemporary and propelled properly by Crewe's own V8. But now, in T form, I fear it has become slightly too powerful. As the lesser R version it offers that instant and utterly unflustered urge that I want in a Bentley, but in the T the sense of indomitability has been replaced by one of dynamic anxiety. For why? The experience of acceleration is always nice – ask an astronaut – but not if, as Bentley himself might have said, it corrupts the overall performance.

It took 8,500,000lb of thrust just to reach the moon, so an extra 93lb ft of torque is neither here nor there. Our own galaxy is 100,000 light years in diameter, so you're going nowhere fast. The nature of the thing is more important, and the numbers alone will lead us only to despair.

But is it too big for this day and age, as some have suggested? I don't think so, but it depends largely on how you see it. There may, after all, be countless other universes in the end of its indicator stalk. At the very least, the whole thing would fit in a thimble.

Cars for art's sake

I can't be the only person in Britain to be worried about the spectre of civic sculpture. The odd Spitfire-on-a-stick is great, and in one or two formerly industrial towns great machines have been preserved as public artworks – printing presses, maybe, or a steam roller. The Angel of t'North is great, but all too often I pass through some urban redevelopment and come away believing that the well-meaning municipal authorities are scrapping an old Dreadnought in the middle of a roundabout.

Round here, though, the problem is statues, apparently. In some areas of West London it is now believed that we already have too many, that there's no room for any more, and that if you've achieved something great but haven't been plinthed yet, it's too late.

More to the point, and as someone close to me might say, who are all these bloody people anyway? After a quick survey of nearby statuary I discover that I am familiar with Queen Victoria and the artist Hogarth, but beyond that it's a load of whiskery old buffoons who probably sent the entire male population of a Welsh mining village to their unnecessary deaths in the space of ten minutes. As at least half of them are celebrated on horseback, they're each occupying a street footprint that could accommodate the new Rolls-Royce convertible, which seems like a better use of the space.

All of this has given me an idea, but it requires the use of a material the name of which I can't remember. Back when I was a lad and Noel Edmonds' Swap Shop and alcopops hadn't been invented, some of my coevals amused themselves with a popular hobby medium called . . . what was it? Plasticraft?* Somebody must remember.

It took the form of a sort of liquid Perspex, which could be poured into small rubbery moulds where it set hard and perfectly clear. If you cast it in two stages, it was possible to seal some curio inside it for all time. Thus boys and girls could preserve an interesting stamp or a first pubic hair for posterity, in the form of a paperweight.

I'm wondering if a whole car could be mounted inside this stuff and put on public display. It's not quite a new idea, as Ferraris have been exhibited in glass boxes in the various piazzas of Firenze, if I remember rightly. But I want something permanent. Various strategic parking spaces around the great cities of Europe should be given over to significant cars locked for ever in . . . whatever it is. Better still, they could go in the places currently occupied by those statues that nobody ever looks at.

Mounting a car in _____ (write the name in if you can remember it) offers several advantages. Before the liquid set, it would completely cover every external and internal surface, protecting it from moisture, oxygen and everything else that might conspire to cause decay. No one would ever steal such a car, because the act of chipping it free would destroy it. For the same reason, unscrupulous classic-car restorers would be prevented from cannibalising the exhibits for that impossible-to-find door mirror or trim piece. People would be able to examine the exhibit in minute detail from a distance of just a few inches, but without ever being able to touch it, and if the _____ ever became scratched, chipped, covered in guano or defaced with graffiti, the council could simply rinse it off and buff it back up to a perfect finish.

---

*Several readers wrote and pointed out that it was called 'Plasticast'.

I can imagine visitors to Britain's towns unexpectedly coming across an Austin 7, a Mini, a Land Rover Defender or a Cortina MkI. I think the French would be into this, too. A Renault 4 and Citroën DS would look great frozen in time in a typical French parking place, which is the pavement or, in the case of the Citroën, the hard shoulder. Imagine a perfect BMW 2002 or Opel Manta simply left by the side of the road but tantalisingly entombed in whatsit. Fine art goes on the wall, great cars should be out on the street, where they look at home.

Motorcycles would also look good in a more upright, narrower transparent prison, slotted between existing parking spaces where you'd expect a motorcycle to be. Bicycles, too: I'm happy to donate my classic Raleigh Superbe three-speed to this community initiative.

Does anyone else think this is a good idea? We've had fish in formaldehyde, it's time for icons of personal transport in whatever that clear plastic is. It will be art if we decide it is.

The domestic cooker – an underrated appliance

No one is more pleased than I am that nature has finally, as the poet Cecil Day-Lewis put it, shaken out the gaudy map of summer. The single stalkless flower of the sun hangs in the inverted bowl of spotless blue, God's in his heaven and all's right with the world. But I've remembered a downside.

Oddly enough, it came to me in the Porsche on an early-evening back-road blast down to Devon. I think the drivers of convertible cars are more attuned than most to the shift in the seasons; to those pheromones of nature that are intensified by forced induction to the inlet tract and reveal Her mood. In the very second that spring flexes a toe under the winter duvet someone, somewhere, in a roofless car will suddenly understand exactly what it was Eleanor Farjeon was on about when she wrote the words for 'Morning Has Broken', and if you drive a convertible you will be the first to hear that distant tap of the wintry drum that so terrified Philip Larkin.

But for now, it's summer, and on the A30 it was unrelenting in its provision of olfactory stimuli. There was the usual stuff: new-mown grass, steaming cow poo, the sweat of a trudging horse at the roadside. The tar itself smelled like the first tar on the first road. I drove past a riotous pub garden and for one fleeting inhalation my lungs were assailed by the heady vapour of fresh gushing beer. I could even smell myself in that strange way one can on the first truly hot day of summer; the gentle searing of forearms and clothing that releases something redolent of the holiday atmosphere of childhood.

But what's this? Something else is burning, and quite badly, too. Oh no. Someone's having a bloody barbecue. The poets were useless. They were right about the rattle of a cuckoo heralding the onset of spring, but they forgot to warn me that summer is ushered in by the sickly stench of an incinerated sausage. The day was ruined and so, too, will England be if we don't act soon to banish the charcoal briquettes menace.

Nothing appetising has ever been cooked on a barbecue, at least in this country. I discover that it's actually a Haitian word, derived from the term used to describe the dried sticks that would form the griddle of one in olden times. And they may have been good at it, being steeped in a culture of outdoor living. But we're not. We are a nation of domestic-appliance obsessives who spend more than most on elaborate ranges from Smeg and Bosch, and are as ill-equipped for primitive living as Titus Oates was for going outside.

The nub of the problem, though, is that barbecues are conducted by men. My proposition here – and I accept that it may be an unfashionable one – is that most men still can't cook. My friends certainly can't, without exception. But in all the couples I know, even though the woman is invariably talented at the stove, 'doing the barbecue' is an inviolable manly duty, just as carving the joint once was. If you're reading this, chaps, well, you know who you are and you're all useless at it.

You stand there, obscured by a pall of smoke, proffering a blazing kebab like a weapon, as if you belonged to some obscure warrior sect sent into the world to rid it of lunch. It doesn't help that it is almost impossible to cook anything properly on a barbecue anyway. It is definitely impossible if the chef has never cooked anything before and regards it as a bonfire. 'Barbecue' is nothing more than a polite euphemism for diarrhoea, and no amount of off-the-shelf couscous will disguise the simple fact that the spare ribs on your paper plate are on fire.

What worries me is that, in a roundabout way, motoring is encouraging this horror. We know the charcoal stuff is only available at petrol stations, and now the sun is up these places are piled high with the hideous 'disposable barbecue', a sort of slotted tin tray ready filled with the material of furious combustion. It would be nice to think that people bought them and immediately threw them away, but they don't. They soak them with paraffin or petrol from the lawnmower, set them alight and then ring me up.

Worse, I see from one of my car magazines that Pininfarina has now produced a gigantic wheeled metal barbecue unit. The Porsche kettle and the Peugeot pepper mill were harmless nonsense, but this is terrifying. It's badged 'Pininfarina' but it's bright red and we all know that really it's a Ferrari barbecue.

Who will buy it? Well, it's well known that any man wearing a Ferrari paddock jacket doesn't actually own a Ferrari. It follows, then, that anyone who buys one of these won't be able to drive it.

The coupé that doesn't cheer

If you've ever been in one of the high-street burger chains, you'll know that the photography they employ around the menu is a bit optimistic. Typically, the depiction of the Double Chodburger will show two glistening patties of plumptious piping hot beef, flyaway curly lettuce and slices of a tomato still in the throes of growth.

The reality is a burger that seems to have been made yesterday with a mangle and then left in direct sunlight. Burger photography must surely be the greatest affront known to modern trade descriptions law. Giant whopper? Not half.

Next in line must be manufacturers' concept cars. I've learned to be similarly suspicious of this stuff over the years.

Consider Jaguar. Every few weeks they show us a new concept, which will be the next F, S, X, Z or K-type. The inside is always modelled on an Art Deco mantle clock and lit like a vodka bar, and it probably plays its own tune. The inside of the real car, though, turns out to be a bit woody, as usual, and with a tasteful analogue clock.

Porsche have been similarly guilty of this. Anyone who put a deposit on the original Boxster on the strength of the show concept must have wondered how they ended up with nothing more than a sports car.

It's even worse in Japan. If you've ever been to the Tokyo Motor Show, you'll have seen whole halls filled with radical city-car concepts inspired by record turntables and the noodle bars of Roppongi, and that can be transformed into a conservatory once parked outside the house. In reality Japan gives us solid, dependable but slightly unimaginative hatchbacks.

My mum bought a Toyota Yaris, a very good car, doubtless. And she was very pleased with it, but only because she'd never been to the Tokyo Show. If she had, she'd have wondered why it didn't hover.

All of which brings me to BMW's Concept CS. Generally, BMW doesn't do too much of this sort of thing, and usually only when it's ready to do business – you may remember the Z8, which stuck to the original motor-show plot when it finally went on sale. I like the look of the CS, which is one of those luxury coupés-that-aren't cars, like Merc's CLS. I know BMW's new-age design has taken a few wonky turns recently, but when it's right – Z4 coupé, 6-Series Cabrio – it's spot on. So the CS is pretty believable, although I'll bet you any money the instruments don't really end up looking like Seeburg jukeboxes.

But I do have a complaint. I think it's going to be too big. Now I like big cars, but generally only when overall bigness translates to a sense of air and space within: Citroën's C8 springs to mind. With these big 'coupés', the impression from inside is often a bit like that felt when living in the ground-floor flat of a 30s mansion block, where the walls are three feet thick to support the weight of the building above, and the windowsills are preposterously deep. You end up feeling slightly cheated, because you've spent all your money on bricks rather than living space. The Mercedes CLS leaves me feeling a bit like that, too. So does *Top Gear* Dog, who appears to be a great beast of a thing, but when you push your fingers into her woolly coat to give her a scratch, you find there's not much actual dog inside.

As has been well documented, cars are much bigger than they used to be, and the current VW Polo is now the size of the original Golf. Why? Why are the doors so thick on new cars? I reckon the doors on my MkI Vauxhall Cavalier were narrower than the door bins on a current Vectra.

Look at the new Alfa Spider. This, too, is a very pretty car, but alongside its 60s forebear it's a great barge of a thing. I know people are growing over time – doorways were lower in Tudor houses, which is why modern people still living in them keep banging their heads, and old beds were very narrow because they only had to accommodate consumptive types raised on a diet of coal. But we haven't changed that much in the last forty years, surely? In any case, the insides of sports cars aren't growing, only the overall dimensions. Comparing a 1963 911 with the current model will show you what I mean.

But for truly damning evidence of this trend, look at the new Best of British range from Matchbox, maker of mere die-cast cars. These are great little models, perfect for a desktop road test and excellent for going sideways.

But you should see the size of the so-called matchboxes they come in. Enormous.

The difficulty of going nowhere

Last week, I went to a place in the British Isles I'd never even heard of. Wigtown. It's somewhere west of Dumfries and round the corner from that bit where the sea juts in, so it's technically in Scotland and therefore abroad. Unless you actually lived in Wigtown, it would be difficult to conceive of a reason for going there. Ever.

I, however, was there to give a talk at the Wigtown Literary Festival on the subject of my latest book, *James May's 20th Century*, which is still available at a number of high-street supermarkets and *Telegraph* Books at an attractively reduced price, yet still not selling half as well as Richard Hammond's autobiography.

Anyway. Wigtown rather surprised me. Firstly, I assumed it would be pronounced 'Whitton', as with some other towns with spellings designed to catch out the plebs (Vale of Belvoir) or the American tourist (Towcester). But no; it really is named after a hairpiece.

Secondly, it's rather like Royston Vasey with a positive spin. It is a local town well served with local amenities run by local people for local people. I gave my talk in the local distillery, was fed by the proprietor of the local bookshop, had a pint in the local pub and was put up for the night by the local farmer, who gave me a bottle of the local whisky afore he went.

The following morning, I was driven back to the railway station by the local doctor. And this was when I was truly bowled over by the place; or, to be more precise, by the quality of the local roads. Wig is not a big town by any standards – I've been in post-office queues with a larger population – but the roads were sweeping, expansive, almost completely empty and altogether superb. And I ended up thinking that if I lived in a place like Wigtown, I'd get up early on a crisp autumnal morning and go for a drive just for the hell of it.

But of course I wouldn't, because I've never been able to do this. Given an interesting new car to try out but, like Chuck Berry, no particular place to go, I'll just drive up the nearby dual carriageway for half an hour and then turn around and come back. I've done this with cars as exciting as the Ferrari F430 and the Maserati Quattroporte, simply because, without a purpose in life, I didn't know what to do with them.

This is a bit of a problem if, like me, you're quite interested in old cars. I have a Fiat Panda for being in other places on time, so the old car is just a hobby, something I drive for fun. But how, exactly, does one drive around 'for fun', even in Wigtown? I've taken Woman out for a drive in the old car before now and got no further than the local jet wash, because that's where my imagination ran out. Of course there have been times when we've decided to go somewhere for the weekend, and you might imagine that this would be an ideal opportunity for 'taking the old girl out for a run'. But because we actually want to get somewhere, we go in the Panda. Regular readers may remember that I recently bought an old Porsche 911. It arrives this weekend and I have no idea what I'm going to do with it. I mean; I've already got a car.

This must be why classic car rallies are so popular. To be honest, I've always avoided such things, imagining that they'd be full of people with otherwise empty lives looking for someone with whom to share concerns about spares availability or ignition advance. Now I realise that without classic car rallies most old cars would never be used, because there's no reason to use them at all in the pursuit of normal life.

So I went on one, the Norwich Union MSA Classic, at the weekend. Driving the Bentley T2 I covered several hundred miles on roads I didn't know existed simply to arrive at Silverstone, wear the tyres out a bit on behalf of the next owner, and come home again. Left to my own devices, I could never have conceived of a route quite so tortuous between my home and the home of British motorsport, but thanks to the supreme efforts of the organisers I was able to spend half a day pursuing a vigorously driven Daf Variomatic through uncharted areas of Berkshire. At the end of the trip I was given a medal – not for putting in a good time, but simply for enjoying a drive around the countryside and eventually arriving at the finishing line.

Brilliant. I could never have done it by myself.

Why we should take heart from car makers

The artificial heart is a marvellous device. At the time of my birth, the real heart beat without hope of relief from man's ingenuity if anything went wrong with it. Its pulse had defined our existence ever since we were aware of having one: its beat was like the bass drum in the rhythm of life, and the day it stopped was the day the music died.

But by 1980 it was possible to implant an artificial one. Looking, and weighing, like something from a Hotpoint spares catalogue, it was powered by compressed air and employed an elaborate system of cams, followers and diaphragms to replicate the muscular contractions of the real thing. And it worked.

I've been handling a selection of artificial hearts in the making of my series on 20th-century wonders, and while it ought to be a rather grisly business, I actually found it quite uplifting. The modern replacement heart is a beautifully miniaturised machine smaller than the real thing and wrought of exotic materials, said by its makers to be good for 100 years of uninterrupted (obviously) service. The notion that it should replicate the pulse has been rejected, and it now functions as a simple pump controlled by a rechargeable battery pack worn on the belt and connected via a tiny socket in the abdomen or even behind the ear.

Here is technology not simply making life easier or more bearable, but actually kicking the reaper up the arse and advising him to come back later. Great stuff.

But here's the rub. One of these hearts can cost in the region of £80,000. Cheap for a life, but still a lot more than most of us have. At this point those of us with healthy tickers can take part in a sponsored bike ride to help raise the cash for some poor bastard who needs the operation, and that's all well and good. But should the price really be that high?

I realise that there are requirements of a new heart that are not shared with the filter in my fish tank, even though the operating principals of the two are very similar. The heart must be what surgeons call 'blood friendly'. The vanes of its impeller must be able to propel the blood at a range of speeds without corrupting its composition or causing it to clot. The mechanism must not be allowed to introduce any contaminant to the crimson fluid, which is why the impeller runs in lubricant-free ceramic bearings or even levitates in the magnetic field that drives it. Access for maintenance is an issue, even compared with the clutch housing on my Honda 500/4, so reliability is everything.

But are the manufacturing requirements of an artificial heart really any more demanding than those of the common-rail injection system in a modern car's diesel engine, which operates at the sort of pressures found in a rifle barrel, whose injector nozzles are made to within tolerances of microns and which can deliver five microscopically measured squirts of fuel in one firing stroke, thousands and thousands of times every hour? A whole diesel car can be yours for under £10,000.

I realise that this might sound a bit fatuous, but it's not meant to. The car is an enduring monument to the industrial process by which something that was once inconceivably complex and temperamental can become accessible to almost everyone at everyone's price. Some parts of the internal combustion engine, the maintenance of which was once a specialised skill in itself, are now sealed and essentially inaccessible. With the car – and for that matter computer hardware and domestic appliances – reliability and low price are driven by a marketplace impulse created by the desire for a more convenient life. With the heart, it's a matter of life itself. But surely that's exactly why the price needs to come down.

And who better to effect a healthy replacement body part price war than those people whose lifeblood – sorry – is the continuous improvement of technological dependability at an ever lower real-world price? The design of the artificial heart is not the issue. The issue is production.

One part of me worries that society takes a perverse thrill in the high cost of anything medical, rather in the way it almost rejoices in a reassuringly expensive solicitor's bill. There is also an economy-of-scale thing at work: artificial hearts are expensive because they are made in small numbers – relatively few people have them. But this was once true of clocks and refrigerators. Maybe fewer people than we'd like have artificial hearts because they are so expensive.

And maybe the motor industry could help.

The car – what were they thinking of?

What my house always needed, more than anything in the world, was a bookcase designed to fill the little redundant niche at the top of the stairs.

This may not sound like much but, believe me, my time on earth would have been more fulfilling and productive if I'd realised. Instead, I put a radiator there and pretty much ruined my life.

Here's the problem. The bookcase, I have calculated, would have accommodated, with space to spare, my sizeable library of works on cars, motorcycles, aeroplanes and World War I. As it is, they're on a set of shelves in my office that was carefully designed to hold all my old vinyl LPs.

So the LPs are in the cupboard in the guest bedroom, which means the protective motorcycle clothing, which is what should be in there, is piled up on top of the small table by the bed. That leaves no room for the portable telly, which lives instead on top of my wardrobe, where, ideally, I'd like to store my suitcases.

So the suitcases live on the floor either on the stairs or by the bed, where I fall over them when carrying a tray of tea and toast to the princess. And so it goes on. This is merely an executive summary of the organisational impasse that has arisen from not having the bookcase.

You might think I'm camping this up a bit but I'm not. The various women who run this place might stand with their hands on their hips telling me I must put this or that pile of detritus away, but they don't realise that they are looking at a model for the chaos that existed before the creation of the universe, and which can be resolved only with a bookcase at the top of the stairs. The knock-on effect of not having one is reverberating through the May household to this day, and is the reason why the washing machine is in the garage. I didn't think it through.

But I still believe I could have made a better job of the early motor car. Recently, I drove a very early Austin 7 Tourer, and was amazed at the paucity of thought applied to the fundamentals of its design.

Now, I know the Austin 7 owners' club will balk at this, and point out that the 7 was Britain's Model T and this nation's first populist car. But it was still pretty terrible. For a start, I'm sure I would have recognised that the peoples' car should have been able to accommodate The People. Why is it so small? Even if the poor really were eating coal, they can't have been that stunted.

I'd also have given it a proper roof, if only because my house had one. I'm sure I would have realised, too, that the door handles should be on the outside. And which bright spark put the cranking handle at the front, thus inviting a car left in gear to run over its owner? It can't have been that difficult to mount it on the side.

There's more. Even the puny radiator of the 7 will burn your hand, so why was it beyond the wit of Herbert and his chums to direct some of that heat to the roofless cabin? It's only a matter of plumbing, and the Romans had that. Yet decades passed before mainstream cars were offered with heaters. Why?

The more I think about it, the more I wonder if the motor industry has ever really known what it was doing. Why did it take so long to work out that the mirrors would be much more effective mounted on the doors than they would be down at the ends of the wings? Why did the interior light and the clock remain expensive options for so long?

Sixty years after its invention, most cars were still groping around in the dark with lights that were barely visible from more than 30 yards away. No one can have thought that big lights were somehow less desirable, so why were they such a long time coming? Engineers and physicists will now write to me to point out that this was all to do with the limitations imposed on the electrical system by the generators and alternators of the time, but hang on. Electricity generation was sorted out in the nineteenth century. The car has progressed painfully slowly.

Consider this. Honda is launching a commercial electric car driven by a 100kW Hydrogen fuel cell, an on-board power station that would run the domestic appliances of my whole street. It's a fascinating development and everyone is suitably impressed.

You might be slightly less impressed, though, as you discover when the fuel cell was invented – 1838.*

---

*Author's note for pedantic science teachers: principle of the fuel cell: Christian Schönbein, 1838. First working fuel cell, William Grove, 1843.

James Bond would like to thank his sponsors

As usual I'm a bit behind with this one, but I've finally seen the new Bond film and I think it's terrific. Low on cheesy special effects, good on snappy dialogue, it's a fairly contemporary take on what Bond should have become by now, and mercifully avoids the tired and inevitable build-up to a denouement in which absolutely everything explodes.

I approve of this Craig bloke as well. Once or twice his dinner jacket wasn't buttoned when I thought it should have been, and I was shocked when he failed to open the passenger door of the old Aston for Vesper and left her to do it for herself. What sort of a role model is that for the men of Britain, most of whom already know more about cooking tiger prawns than about government-issue side arms and their calibres? But apart from that I'd say yes, Mr Bond, I expect you to survive for quite a bit.

And, although this may seem a strange thing to say in a motoring column, I was pleased there was no car chase. I've never quite bought in to the cult of the cinematic car chase. There's always been something slightly unconvincing about two floppy American cars bouncing around San Francisco, or a slightly speeded-up DB5 roaring about in a disused warehouse. Instead, we get fantastic and protracted pursuits on foot, and even if two men leaping between vertiginously high structures (cranes, in this case) always invokes the cable-car scene from *Where Eagles Dare*, it's still more impressive than driving through a pile of cardboard boxes.

Great stuff. Proper family entertainment with no swearing or nudity, as my mum might say. However, and with the inevitability of a baddie with metal body parts being electrocuted at some point, here comes a complaint.

I'm becoming rather tired of product placement. It begins with whatever mobile phone it is he uses, which looms large on the screen seemingly once every five minutes. If you're the man or woman responsible for brokering the deal by which this was achieved, I'd like to assure you, with some smugness, that I never actually noticed what make it was. Ha!

Cut to a truly nauseating bit on a train when Bond tells us his watch is an Omega. I could almost here the crump of money landing on the production desk. What worries me is that I have a similar Omega, and I think I may have to sell it in case anyone thinks I bought it 'because James Bond has one'. I already have an LED digital watch from the 70s that I bought because James Bond had one.

And then there are the cars. I think one of the bad guys may have been seen near a Volga, which pleased me immensely. It's nice to know that the prejudices engendered by the Cold War have been swept away everywhere except in our innate sense of what a man with a scar on his face should drive. But other than that, it was largely an *homage* (film critic's term, that) to Ford's Premier Automotive Group.

There was the Aston, obviously, and lots of Jaguar badges and grilles moving through the frame, plus a Volvo or two, and a 'coming soon' moment with the new 2007 Mondeo. 'James Bond is driving a Ford!' said Woman, incredulously, as the Mondeo crashed through shot from screen left, and probably pulled up next to an XC90. She had a point. I know he's been seen in small Renaults and Citroëns before, but this seemed particularly un-Bond. I expected Jeremy Clarkson to climb out and talk about the torque of the V6 version.

And never mind the stakes at the card table. I'd like to have been in on the bidding war for the car parking spaces outside, especially for the elevated shot in which even the producer seemed to have lost his bottle slightly. One of the cars was a Bentley Continental GT, made by VW. This was obviously agreed on the understanding that a Jag would roll up as well, as indeed it did.

Do they imagine we don't know what's going on here? Maybe this sort of thing really works on a subliminal level. Maybe other people don't really notice it. But to me, sitting in row 37 seat B in my role as May, James May, the whole business quickly became annoying. In fact, I began to feel as though I'd paid £9 to sit and watch a very, very lengthy advertisement, and wondered when the film would start.

Still, there's a fairly simple solution. The Bond theme is becoming a bit tired anyway, so they may as well change it for a new tune: pah-pah, pah-pah, pah-pah, pah-paaaaaah . . .

. . . Pah!

Harley-Davidson, hardly appropriate

I write to you this week from sunny California, where I will be for a whole month, ostensibly working on the next series of *Oz and James's Big Wine Adventure*. However, as no one will ever believe that this is work, I may as well admit now, and especially to myself, that I'm on holiday.

It's easy, really. I drive along in a huge 42-foot-long mobile home (more of this soon), soothed by the thrum of its lazy industrial diesel engine and the constant rattle of a 120 year old man talking about the wind on the hills and the struggle of the vine, and at my destination I try a Rhone Valley derivative made by some nutcase who gave up a promising career in medicine or IT to be at one with the earth. All I have to do is make some vaguely intelligent comment about the woody high notes and brace myself for a tirade of dismissive abuse from the wine ponce. Then it's back to the 'bago for some traditional British motorhome cooking. It's brilliant.

But, as ever, America, and California in particular, leaves me slightly 'conflicted', as the trick cyclists would say. On one hand, I truly love the place – the mountains that form the constant and immovable backdrop to our progress, the sense that it's almost a desert, the microbrewery beer, Cheez Whiz, the undertone of respectable intellectual anarchy and the distinct impression that everyone here has, at some time, been on the *Bob Hope*. The impression of infinite space is nice, too, especially when trying to reverse the rig.

On the other hand, there's Barney's Beanery, a popular bar and restaurant in downtown LA. When I walked in, I couldn't understand why everyone was reading a broadsheet newspaper. But then I realised that it was, of course, the menu. It was the same size as the *Telegraph* motoring section but two pages longer, and the number of dishes certainly numbered over 300 and were all available with extra beans or strawberries, add 50 cents. Everything was huge, of course, and even the entry-level 'cup' of clam chowder was served in a skinless orchestral timpani. The whole experience was, as Oz put it, a bit like having an American coffee, in that you're never sure that you're having one at all. America can seem like a land of incredible and inexhaustible plenty devoid of any actual flavour.

Which sort of brings me to the thorny subject of Harley-Davidson motorcycles. Back home, I've never really bought in to the H-D thing, partly because the bike is only the start of it. It also includes the clothing, the luggage, the Harley-Davidson corkscrew, the aftershave and the Harley-Davidson condoms, all there in the interests of providing an entire off-the-peg existence. In Britain, Harleys seem to be ridden by people who secretly wish they'd been born American. My friend Richard Hammond recently bought a Harley, but he already had a big hat and some cowboy boots so he probably thought he might as well keep going.

I've never really been able to keep pace with the Harley range, either. I can just about recognise the Electra Glide and the V-Rod, but there's also the Hardtail, the Night Rod, the Dyno Rod, the Chop Job, the Bob Job, the Custom Billy Bob Jnr, the Big Boy, the Bad Lad and the Fat Bastard. As in Barney's, there is an endless list of extras, with the result that Harley-Davidson varietals are complex, robust and exhibit an extremely expensive finish.

So no thanks. And yet ... there are thousands of Harleys thudding their way around California; they are parked up in the trailer parks where we stay, lugged across the country in

Winnebagos and then rolled out for a spot of local cruising. And for some reason, I'm having incredibly lustful thoughts about them.

The Bob-a-Job Choptail has never seemed so beautiful, with its proudly exposed cylinder fins, its indulgent chrome adornments, the swell of its teardrop tank, the agricultural vastness of its footboards and frame tubes, and everything else that makes it look so ridiculous in Hammersmith. Out here it resonates perfectly with the mountains in the infinite distance and the futility of trying to go anywhere quickly rather than at leisure, and suddenly it's blokes on Japanese sports bikes who look horribly misguided. I find myself gagging for a ride on a Harley, just as I suddenly decide that, yes, I will have something called 'Liquid Smoke' on my New York Strip steak. I'd never do that at home.

It may be the drink, I suppose, since, as W.B. Yeats observed, 'Wine comes in at the mouth, and love comes in at the eye'. Hopefully, this is just a classic holiday romance, and once I return home I'll get over it.

Won't I?

The biggest spanner in the world

An aspect of the internal combustion engine that has long baffled car enthusiasts, and even some car journalists, is that of torque.

A lot of people, dieselists in particular, are fond of talking about torque without really knowing what it is. It is generally understood that a lot of torque makes a car feel muscular, and that big engines give more torque than small ones. This is broadly true, but what is torque, exactly? Well, I pride myself on understanding it, and that, of course, means I'm heading for a fall somewhere towards the end of this column.

In essence, torque is a force at a distance; hence the units, which are usually lb ft in Britain. A one-pound weight at one end of a one-foot rod pivoted at the other end produces a torque of 1lb ft. This is sometimes also known as a 'turning moment', and for obvious reasons.

Torque is also sometimes known as 'twist action' in the motoring vernacular, and it's a good way to describe it. The crankshaft of the engine is like the pivot in the illustration above, and if it developed 1lb ft of torque it would be able to lift the weight.

Torque, then, is a sort of leverage, and is nothing new. 'Give me a place to stand and a lever long enough,' said Archimedes in 220BC, 'and I will move the world.'

In other words, if you can't shift a boulder with your shoulder, you could do it with a lever. The longer your lever, the easier it is to shift. But the longer your lever, the less distance you will move it for a given effort. The lever multiplies the torque but at the expense of speed.

Since we've got this far, we may as well consider the gearbox en route to the revelation that I don't really understand torque at all and have misapplied it with ruinous consequences for my motoring life.

The gearbox in a car is nothing more than a series of levers in circular form. A low gear is a long lever in the boulder analogy, and so the car will accelerate more easily. But it won't now go as fast as it will in top gear. The gearbox allows the driver to trade pure grunt and pure speed in the constantly shifting dynamics market that is the need to accelerate, cruise, climb hills and tow caravans. I'm afraid I find this sort of thing terribly interesting.

But, ultimately, I'm still a bit thick. Let us now move to my garage, where the Honda 500/4 has been needing some new clutch plates. In order to get at the clutch cover, I had to remove one of its exhaust pipes. You needn't worry too much about the details of this job, so we'll fast forward to that point near the end of the operation, where everything is mended and I have only to reaffix the pipe.

At the engine end, it is secured by two nuts on short threaded studs protruding from the cylinder head. I lined everything up, screwed the nuts on to finger-tightness, then took out the big socket wrench to give them a good tighten.

I gave one a couple of turns, and then the other. A bit at a time. Make sure it's evenly seated. Now just a final 'nip up' and . . . bang! One of the studs sheared off.

Other misguided amateur mechanics will already have guessed where this was going to end. They will know, also, that the human condition cannot ebb to a point lower than that instant of intense misery in which something on an old motorcycle breaks under excessive force. Every other failure and inadequacy of your life to date seems to reverberate in the clatter of the tool across the floor, and then you sit motionless for an age in the silent garage, alone save for the slavering black dog of your despair. It is the only time I have wished for the company of Jeremy Clarkson and his predictable suggestion that I should 'just hit it with a hammer'.

Here are the hard facts. The wrench is about two feet long, and I had probably applied a force of about 60lb to the end of it. That's a torque of 120lb ft, which, curiously, is pretty much the output of the 2.0-litre petrol engine in the VW Sharan. If I'd thought about it that way, I'd have realised that I didn't need a large people-carrier to tighten a 10mm nut on a 34-year-old and slightly crusty exhaust stud. But I didn't, and now everything's ruined.

A little learning is a dangerous thing. And I've never actually known who said that.

Brown must go

A few years back, I lamented the revival of brown as an acceptable colour for a car. I think I had just driven a VW that was finished in Evening Beige or some such.

Brown, I reasoned, was an unsuitable colour for a car because it is not one we associate with motion. Trees and fields are brown, depictions of space rockets in science-fiction comics are red or white. Brown is good for organic matter where it is infinitely varied in hue and texture, which is why it looks good on conkers and Labradors. It even looks good in the interior of my Porsche, because it's brown leather and delightfully mottled like a nicely aged chukka boot. But in a solid and unrelenting form, such as paint, it doesn't work, and especially not on anything intended to invoke a desire for movement. I live quite near an airport and am fairly certain that no respectable airline has chosen brown for its corporate livery.

And it obviously wasn't just me, because, three years on, the threatened brown-car renaissance has not, after all, exploded onto our roads like the effluent from a ruptured council sewage tanker.

But it might yet. In the last few weeks I've once again noticed a few obviously very new and undeniably very brown cars out there. One of them was a Bentley, for Pete's sake. Someone has parked a brown car around the corner from my house, and the whole street has been plunged into gloom and despair by the way it sucks in all light and proper colour from the formerly pleasant urban scene. And now a friend has expressed an interest in ordering a small Japanese hatchback in 'something chocolatey', and she didn't mean Milky Bar.

This really must stop, and I've come up with an even better reason why a car should not be brown. Cars are technologically more forward-looking than they've been at any time in their short history, and brown is absolutely not the colour of progress.

This much struck me while visiting a rather interesting museum of early domestic radios while working on my series about twentieth-century technology. The incongruity apparent in early radios is that although they were the technical marvel of the age, they still ended up looking like 300-year-old furniture. The tuning scale, glowing warmly like some futuristic hearth for the comfort of the assembled and astonished family, was set in wood, and wood is almost always brown.

Early gramophones and televisions were wooden, and hence brown, as well. Even their knobs and switches, though they may seem black at first, will, on closer examination, be revealed to be of Bakelite and hence very dark brown. Same goes for the first domestic telephones. Worse still, all of these things were additions to the progressive home, not replacements for anything. So they merely added to the overwhelmingly brown theme long established by tables and sideboards. Brown is, in a way, symbolic of these early devices' struggle to attain true modernity.

Because in the pre-modern world, surely everything was brown. It was largely mud anyway, and mud is brown. Pre-war pubs have brown tiled floors and brown panelled walls. Old wallpaper was brown. When coal was burned the air itself could turn slightly brown. The world was dirtier then and dirt is inevitably brown and was everywhere. The poet Philip Larkin acknowledged that your life would be screwed up by your parents, but that theirs had been screwed up in turn by 'fools in old-style hats and coats'. I've seen photographs of the sort of people he was referring to, and though the photographs may be black and white, I can tell from some spectral resonance of the greys that those hats and coats were often brown, too. People must have thought in brown back then.

But with modernity and new materials such as plastic, nylon, synthetic rubbers and composites, technological pioneers were no longer obliged to use brown and, as optimists, didn't. The rise of the transistor radio, and its consequent miniaturisation, roughly coincided with the advent of injection-moulded plastics. You will struggle to find a 1950s pocket radio in anything other than red, yellow or bright blue. This was the age in which the cult of radio really took off; in short, when it was released from brown bondage.

Quite right too. Think of some of the modern things that people are buying at the moment: computers, iPods, plasma televisions, juicers, high-tech training shoes, carbon-fibre skis, mobile phones. I haven't seen any brown examples, and the same goes for any new aeroplane, railway locomotive or speed boat.

The future is always bright; it might even be orange. But it will never be brown, and neither should your car.

I saw the light, and saw that it was poor

Until now, the darkest hotel I've ever stayed in was the Hotel Borg in Reykjavik. I believe it is the oldest hotel in the city, an Art Deco masterpiece retaining a wealth of period decorative features that guests will appreciate if they happened to bring a torch.

But now I'm in the Hudson Hotel in Manhattan and, God in heaven, it's dim. The combined wattage of all the light fittings in the lobby is just about equal to that of a Pifco bicycle lamp. There is a generous skylight above the main reception desk, and during the morning it might flood the whole floor with God's recreation of the new day, except that the management has trained a thick creeper to grow all over it, thus condemning the staff and residents to eternal night.

It was worse when I eventually groped my way to my bedroom. Yes, there were lights on in there, but not the sort intended to illuminate anything. Call me unromantic, but in a room I'm only going to use once I'm a fan of what I still call 'the big light': that is, a single bulb-and-flex type arrangement hanging from the ceiling and operated by an obvious switch by the door, of at least 150 watts and preferably bare, so that Edison's vision of instant and constant light can arrive at my eyeball uninterrupted.

Instead, there was clever-dick stuff in corners and behind bedsteads, all worked by switches disguised as tassels or heating controls. I hate this sort of thing. I climb into bed but by the time I've managed to switch everything off it's time to get up again.

However, and unusually, I didn't stay there for one night. I stayed for four whole days, and by the end of the second I was beginning to enjoy not being able to see properly. Instead of the insistence of all-pervading light, I enjoyed the gentle retinal titillation of countless glittering pinpricks and feeble coloured globes. It was all really quite magical, like combining Christmas with pleasure.

Sadly, my own knowledge of interior lighting does not really extend beyond the car, although I can see that in the car there is much work to be done. I've complained before that all but a few car interiors are awful and fashioned from materials that no sane person would use in the home. But maybe all can be saved with the mystical properties of mood lighting.

In my own motoring life, it was a Bentley that first seemed to bow to the influence of the John Lewis home lighting department. In the roof above the Arnage's facia is a tiny orange bulb, there to lend the plated switches in the cabin a warmth and softness. It really works. Cover it with your finger and see how much more industrial your environment suddenly feels.

BMW does something similar in the new Mini, only now you can change the colour to suit your temperament. VW have given us spooky blue dials and Alfa Romeo, in the 164, made the main interior light like something normally found under the water of a swimming pool. But there's room for more.

A while back I met a neon bender – this is the accepted name for someone versed in the delicate art of creating neon signs. What I knew of neon was that it glows red, while argon glows blue. But the bender showed me that by combining these gasses with tinted glass and phosphorescent coatings, all sorts of subtle and gentle colours could be created. How about some neon tubes in footwells? And how about something like a disco ball or magic lantern, projecting flashes of light or occult symbols across the seats and door panels?

I realise that some of you will be ready to dismiss me as a slightly whoopsie would-be *World of Interiors* commentator, but I know I'm on to something because this sort of stuff, like electric windows and air-con, starts at the top and works its way downwards. And as you may well know, the Rolls-Royce 101EX concept has, where other makers would put a head-lining, the sky at night.

It's a simple idea, a myriad holes over a diffused light source to give an impression of the Milky Way. And I know it's also an old one, and has featured in countless hen-night stretched limos. But I would allow customers to specify their own arrangements of stars, so that the Plough, Orion and the Bear might come together in a way never permitted by the celestial clockwork; to add the moon, too, and maybe a fictional comet or two.

Then I would sit back, relax and, like W.B. Yeats, think of my past greatness when a part of the constellations of heaven.

Australians singing in shower – world will end

One of the things that really annoys me about environmentalists is that I've never met a genuine one. Obviously, some of my leftwing friends are driving around in small diesel hatchbacks claiming to be concerned about CO2 emissions, but the truth is that they'd drive them anyway, because they're not interested.

Recycling is another one. We have a recycling scheme where I live, and I approve of it: re-using material instead of chucking it in a hole in the ground is a good principle at the very least. But let's be honest here. All we are really doing is putting the same rubbish in a different-coloured bag. I've never re-used an empty Spam tin as a flower pot or anything like that.

In short, no one I know has abandoned anything he or she holds dear in the name of saving the environment. Anyone who genuinely believes that planet earth is the most important thing in the world should make a stand against human reproduction, since babies must represent the pollution of the future. But only Philip Larkin was miserable enough to suggest that people shouldn't have kids (and he was, by the way, something of an environmentalist).

Instead, we're subjected to a lot of fatuous cobblers about the environmental burden of keeping a television on standby or leaving a light on somewhere. Recently, I read some research – an insult to arithmetic, really – that purported to demonstrate how much global warming was being caused by

Australians singing in the shower. Do we honestly believe that Bruce and Sheila should not be allowed to join in a verse or two of *Waltzing Matilda* once a month?

The fact is that human advancement has gone hand in hand with an increase in energy consumption ever since primitive man first built a bonfire and smelted some ore to make a spear tip. I honestly don't see how we can go backwards, and I really don't want to see the sky blackened by giant windmills, so I've decided to join the pro-nuclear lobby.

Surely, if we apply all the effort that's being expended on phoney environmentalism to making nuclear power safe and dependable, we can have limitless energy. Nuclear power stations can be used to fuel the anticipated hydrogen infra-structure – hydrogen really being little more than an efficient way to store electricity – and we can be in the happy position of running our homes from the on-board power stations in our fuel-cell cars, instead of imagining we will recharge electric cars from the mains supply of the home, which may well be generated using fossil fuel anyway.

But no. Instead I find myself being lectured about, for example, the environmental benefits of eating seasonal domestic produce. Those of us with any sense have always done this anyway, because it's one of life's great pleasures. It's hardly a new idea.

And then I'm subjected to a righteous plea from someone with supposedly green credentials to stop using supermarket carrier bags. Those of us with half an ounce of sense never did. They're ugly, they blow around on windy days, and they make any man look downtrodden and emasculated. We already know that a wicker two-handled bag is more voguish for a lady, and that a military-style duffel bag or rucksack is more becoming of a gentleman. Those of us who realise this have been polythene-neutral for decades.

Finally, there's that old chestnut, the bicycle. In London, where I live, the mayor has taken to slapping up giant posters (at a considerable price in CO2, I imagine) telling me that 'it's better by bike'. The other day, a newspaper interviewer, talking to me about the future of the car, asked 'What about bicycles?'.

Do these people imagine we have never heard of bicycles? Or that we have no idea what they're good for? I haven't been without one since I was three, and I still use one regularly. There are few things I find more galling than to be confronted by a man who bought a bicycle last week and harangued about their benefits, as if the bloody thing's only just been invented and no one else has quite cottoned on to it yet.

When I cycle down to the end of my road en route to the local seasonal greengrocers with my reusable duffel bag, I don't need a poster to tell me I'm doing the sensible thing. I've known for years. Similarly, if I turn out of the road in my car heading for Scotland, there's no point trying to convince me I'd be better off going on a bicycle, because I've actually done that and I can assure you it's not true.

Environmentalists – stop treating us like idiots. The rest of you, relax. It's OK to own a car.

Once more, with feeling

When I had my first car, I was perfectly happy to drive along for hours on end singing to myself. Of course I was. It was a MkI Vauxhall Cavalier, the L model, with no radio. It's almost unthinkable now.

But the other day, I briefly disconnected the battery in one of my old cars and then realised I didn't have the security code that brings the radio back to life. And so, for the first time in several decades, I was forced to rely on the oral tradition.

Now it's been demonstrated that singing is good for you, so singing in the car is nothing to be ashamed of. I know plenty of people who do it when an old favourite comes on Radio 2. One man I know also has an invisible drum kit in the car, and plays it while waiting at traffic lights.

So, this being the season etc, as I drove along wirelesslessly, I decided to see how many Christmas carols I could remember. I hadn't done any carol singing all year, and the car seemed like a good place for it. It may in fact be the only place, as public carol singing has now almost certainly been made illegal in Britain.

All went well. I could do all of 'Oh come . . .', including the descant, and most of 'Hark the herald . . .' and 'Once in Royal . . .'. But then I had a go at 'The Holly and the Ivy' and remembered something that has bothered me since I was a boy, and which I think I have now cleared up. Everyone gets 'The Holly and the Ivy' wrong.

A bit of background. This carol is one of the many songs collected by the unrepentant folkist Cecil Sharp back at the beginning of the last century, but the melody and much of the text are a great deal older than that. Its origins are pagan, holly and ivy being both symbols of winter hardiness to inspire the peasants and, inevitably, something to do with fertility. And without wishing to be too Radio 3 about this, the melody sounds to me as though it is rooted in medieval plainsong.

And that may be at the root of the problem: the whole thing is, metrically, a bit wonky. Even in the first verse:

> The holly and the ivy
> When they are both full grown
> Of all the trees that are in the wood
> The holly bears the crown.

The ancient lyric doesn't really fit the tune without resorting to an 'o-of' and a 'the-e' and turning 'that are' into a single word. I was reminded of this while sitting in some roadworks on the A316.

In the refrain, though, everything can go completely to pot. The text makes perfect sense written down but in the singing tends to come out as:

> Oh the rising of the su-un
> Andtherunning of the deer
> The-e playing of the merry or
> Gnsweet singing in the choir.

This is what drives me up the wall. I appreciate that the original may have become corrupted by the inadequacies of the art of example between its conception and the point when Sharp heard an old woman sing it in Sodding Chipbury, but how the hell did the second half of 'organ' ever become fastened to the beginning of 'sweet'?

Back home, to be absolutely certain of my ground, I consulted the dictionary. No – there is no such word as 'gnsweet' in the English language. No one has ever ordered gnsweet and sour pork from a Chinese takeaway and the Searchers certainly never sang of 'Gnsweets for my gnsweet, sugar for my honey', so there's no excuse for it in this ancient wassail. Unless, of course, it's a word that existed in 1250 but has since fallen out of use. Like, for example, 'wassail'. I've checked that as well, and it isn't.

But still thousands of people turn up at midnight mass or the school carol concert and blithely perpetrate the myth that the choir is singing gnsweetly while some bloke plays along on the 'or', when by the simple expedient of singing 'of' and 'the' to the same note in line three of the refrain, the merry organ can be fully assembled before the choir even turns up. This is how I think it should be.

A quick trawl through versions of 'The Holly and the Ivy' on iTunes reveals that this Christmas conundrum is as vexing for professionals as it is for your casual in-car caroler. A group called the Mediaeval Baebes take the unprecedented step of replacing the organ entirely, with a merry harp. No one is fooled. A Disney rendition talks of the playing of the pretty flute, which is just Mickey Mouse. Meanwhile, even the choir of St Paul's Cathedral falls into the gnsweet trap on their album *Christmas Carols from St Paul's*, released in 1994.

But, joy to the world, the choir of King's College, Cambridge, under Sir David Wilcox, get it right on their 2005 album, *Essential Carols – The Very Best of King's College, Cambridge*. This, then, is the one you should buy.

I'm glad that's sorted. This Christmas, let's see if we can all sing from the same carol sheet.

No jam tomorrow

I don't know if anyone ever sent you – or if you even noticed it amongst all the offers of a bigger penis, the opportunity to invest in Nigeria, or something called 'Monday morning humour' – that round-robin email about the anti road-pricing petition.

Here's how it worked. Downing Street's website – where anyone can create a petition – had one on which you could register your objection to a form of tax that researchers say will burden some school-run mothers with a bill for £86 a month. But they didn't exactly advertise it, because if more than 750,000 names are logged on a petition, they are constitutionally obliged to look into it.

By the time you read this, it will be too late, because the deadline for responding was the beginning of March. And that would have been the end of that, were it not for whoever created the world's first genuinely useful circular email. When I looked this morning – still well within the cut-off date – 1,114,156 people had registered a digital gypsy's warning to Mr Brown and his evil henchmen. By lunchtime, Radio 2 could reveal that another 200,000 or so had been added. Hoorah for desktop democracy.

Unfortunately, though, and as we know from the miners' strike, the poll-tax riots, the anti-war march and those people who hang around outside McDonalds with leaflets about vegetarianism, protest doesn't really work. At least, not unless it involves a truly significant portion of the population, as it did in the General Strike, the women's suffrage movement, and Indian passive resistance. Even if the road-pricing petition closes with three million signatories, it's still an insignificant portion of the total driving population of Britain.

I have therefore come up with a better idea, which I am incorporating into the fledgling manifesto of a new governmental system known as May's Britain. More of this on another day, since it's rather complex and involves the summary imprisonment of around 80 per cent of the population, including, I suspect, Clarkson and Hammond. But here's the thinking behind this bit.

Yes, we will pay to use the roads. We already do, of course, through road tax and petrol duty, but we will allow pay-as-you-go road pricing as well. Road space is a finite commodity and so, the economics argument would go, it must have a value. Fair enough.

But if any part of our road is unavailable to us, we receive a massive refund.

This makes perfect sense. If the local council decided to widen the pavement outside my house and wanted a few feet out of my front yard, they'd have to buy it from me. It's my yard, I paid for it, so it comes at a price.

The other day I retiled my bathroom floor. As I hadn't bothered to measure it, I bought more than enough tiles from the shop. When, at the end of the operation, I still had a whole box left, the shop bought them back from me.

Only yesterday I cancelled the insurance on one of my cars, which I've just sold. As I'd paid for a year's cover and only used three months' worth, the insurance company duly sent me a cheque for the difference. No one would regard this as anything other than fair and reasonable.

This brings me, inevitably, to the subject of roadworks. I've just spent an hour driving along one lane of the A316 dual carriageway into London, the other one being closed for a distance of some five miles. It was a Sunday evening, and tens of thousands of people desperate to return home to their loved ones and *Top Gear* were horribly inconvenienced. And yes, as you've probably guessed, there was not a single person, wheelbarrow, or abandoned mug anywhere to be seen within the area closed to protect the workforce.

I know this complaint is as old as the car itself. I know that every single road user in the country would agree that closing the road and then not doing anything with it is insultingly stupid. I've a good mind to start a petition. But then, there's no point in simply objecting, because that didn't stop the invasion of Iraq so it certainly won't persuade a lot of local government numpties to stop eating biscuits and get on with their work. A proper incentive, based on jeopardy, is required.

And let's not blame the workers. Clarkson, Hammond and I spent twenty-four hours with some of them recently, and they're a stout bunch of chaps. Their work is quite hazardous, they go to it with a will (when the Tarmac eventually arrives) and they want to go home as much as anyone else. No, the problem is somewhere with t' management.

In an earlier incarnation of May's Britain, everyone involved in the failure to organise roadworks properly would simply be in prison. The thought of them slopping out, however, is not that much of a comfort when you're stuck in the jam they've created.

I also thought about resurrecting those cages used in olden times, the ones suspended from trees and derricks, where they put highwaymen and pirates so that the people could be entertained watching them starve. Roads managers would be locked in one of these as the first bollard was placed and not allowed to come out until the last one was put away.

But this wouldn't work for ever. Imagine the Oxford ring, where the road works have been going on for years. The roadside trees would be decked with hundreds of rotting executives, and I suspect that by now Oxfordshire's commuters would be bored with running odds on which eyeball would be the next one to be pecked out by a crow.

No – the rebate system is the answer. The instant work stops on any coned-off stretch of road, the man in charge has to stand at its end, naked save for his hard hat, and hand out money to drivers. Let's say a pound for every extra minute the journey has taken compared with an average time when the road is clear.

So on my trip along the A316, I'd have collected around £45 in return for not being able to drive on road that I've already paid for. And so would every other driver on that Sunday evening. It might easily come to a million pounds. Let's see how long they shilly-shally around with that sort of disincentive hanging over them.

You know it makes sense. It's just one more reason why May's Britain is the sort of place you'd want to live.

Index